Sailing on Ice

Photo by Derek Williamson, *Hunterdon* (N.J.) *Review.*

Sailing on Ice

Jack Andresen

South Brunswick and New York: A. S. Barnes and Company
London: Thomas Yoseloff Ltd

A. S. Barnes and Co., Inc.
Cranbury, New Jersey 08512

Thomas Yoseloff Ltd
108 New Bond Street
London W1Y OQX, England

Library of Congress Cataloging in Publication Data

Andresen, Jack.
Sailing on ice.

1. Ice-boats.   I. Title.
GV843.A52   796.9'7   73-101
        ISBN 0-498-01241-7

First printing, August, 1974
Second printing, October, 1976

PRINTED IN THE UNITED STATES OF AMERICA

Contents

Acknowledgments

I am deeply indebted to my many friends in the iceboating world who have taught me how to sail and have given so generously of their time and effort in club organization, regatta officiating, and helping with my equipment. Among these were Pres Schreve, Walt Pilcer, Willi Schmitz, Homer Sieder, and Jay Dowling. I am particularly grateful to my dear wife, Evelyn, who encourages me in the sport, loves to ride herself, and prepares such delicious hot meals after a day on the ice.

Introduction

This book acquaints you with an iceboat and helps you sail it better. Some iceboaters sail for the pure exhilaration of speed on the broad ice areas, unconfined to narrow roads as is a motorcycle or sports car. These people often prefer a larger boat to be able to share their thrills with friends. For others, the competition at a regatta or in club racing is what makes the sport. A competitive sailor does not have to win to enjoy a race. He does, however, have to feel he is improving his skill; the race is his measure of improvement. A novice, even though he may say that he races just for the fun of it, is thrilled by moving up from last to next to last. Then one day, posssibly with good luck, he actually finishes near the winners. After that he is hooked!

Iceboating has two competitive aspects: making a better machine and sailing it better in a race. In the Skeeter class, the machine can be changed within broad limits thus offering a challenge to the inventive craftsman. In the Arrow class, a strict "one-design" class, modifications are not permitted but keeping the craft in perfect condition plays a part in winning a race.

Most competitive sports are dominated by youth, but ice sailing is a noteworthy exception. The patience required when a race is postponed due to poor ice or wind demands a degree of maturity. The skill and judgment needed to win a race cannot be acquired quickly. Five seasons of racing are just a beginning; champion ice racers over fifty are not rare.

In this book techniques are described with front-steering ice-boats in mind, because the trend is definitely toward this type. However, the stern steerers and Scooters are not dead. The big stern steerers, which can hold up to a dozen people, are still used and loved. The Scooter proponents are a special breed of sportsmen for whom a Scooter is still the greatest thing on ice.

With more people becoming interested in iceboating, innovations and possibly completely new designs will arise. We can expect welded-steel frames, rigid airplane-wing type sails, venetian-blind type sails, four-runner hulls, and new types of runners. All of these old ideas will be retried and possibly be successful in combination with new ones.

About semantics—the terms *ice yacht* and *iceboat* are synonymous. An iceboat is a cross between a sailplane and a boat; for this reason the terminology embraces both the aviation and the nautical jargon. We refer to the *nose* or the *bow*, the *tail* or *stern*, the *fuselage* or the *hull*, upwind or to weather downwind or alee, left or port, etc. For other terminology, please refer to the glossary and make your own choice.

Iceboating requires a sheet of reasonably smooth ice, not less than 2½ inches thick, and an area of at least one-half mile square, although more is much better. Of course, you also need wind. Having one without the other has driven more than a few enthusiasts to utter impolite words, most surely offending the deity in charge of these things.

In areas where ice is found there is usually also wind—but its speed varies widely during the day and from one day to the next. Generally, wind is lowest at dawn and dusk and picks up during the middle of the day. So, when you have both, don't stand and talk—sail!

A perfectly aligned yacht can sail in as little as 3 knots of wind on perfect ice. But good racing wind is from 5 to 21 knots (6 to 24 mph). Higher wind can be exciting and give tremendous speeds, but as one knowledgeable wag put it, "They go fastest just before they fall apart."

Conditions suitable for iceboating exist over the Northeast and north central United States and adjacent sections of Canada. In continental Europe suitable conditions exist in northern France, Germany, Holland, Belgium, Denmark, and the Baltic Sea coastal areas up to Leningrad. There are undoubtedly many areas in which good conditions exist but where iceboats have not been introduced. The high plateau areas such as in the western U.S., northern Japan and the

U.S.S.R., where there is cold weather and low precipitation, are possibilities for extension of the sport.

Humorist, author and newspaper reporter, Dereck Williamson, of the *Hunterdon Review*, Whitehouse Station, N.J., described his first iceboat ride as follows:

> Going more than 60 mph in a sailboat is a lot of fun, if you don't mind the pieces of ice in your teeth.
>
> You've also got to watch out for the old Christmas trees.
>
> On Saturday, the sport of iceboating came to the reservoir, which is frozen over in some spots.
>
> For the expert, it's an exciting, demanding, and often hairy sport.
>
> For the novice, it's the same thing plus downright confusing. Like the Christmas trees.
>
> "What are all the Christmas trees for?" I asked on Saturday morning, as guys wearing insulated boots and spiked ice creepers and insulated coveralls and face masks and helmets and goggles were taking a bunch of trees and boats from station wagons.
>
> "We put them out there on the ice to mark the spots of open water," said a man in red coveralls with a shoulder patch that read "Don't Eat Yellow Snow."
>
> As a newspaper reporter, I felt pretty silly. I mean, what a logical answer. And what a great way to make use of old Christmas trees!
>
> The man in red had set the race course—two flags about a mile and a half apart. The 17 slim racing craft now being assembled at the edge of the reservoir would sail around the flags three times. Four races were to be sailed, and similar events on Sunday would constitute a regatta.
>
> One boat was coming in, fast. It wheeled around into the wind and the skipper or pilot or whatever you call somebody who runs an iceboat pulled a lever and a sticklike thing scraped along the ice with a loud scraping sound and the boat stopped. The boat was named *Skidoo*.
>
> A man wrapped up like a mummy climbed out, and ducked under the flapping sail. Somebody said it was Jack Andresen, Eastern Arrow Champion.
>
> Arrow is the name of the boat, a two-place, 250-pound boat with about 70 square feet of sail area. Bigger than a DN and smaller than a Yankee and a Skeeter.
>
> Jack invited me to go for a ride in his Arrow, and as we walked out on the ice he explained that waterskiing used to be his thing, but that iceboating was his thing now.
>
> "It's not a new sport; there are about, say 5,000 iceboats. The most popular, about 3,000 of them, are the DNs, which are also the smallest. It's an Eastern Division race, and we're anxious to see how this reservoir is. It's the first time for iceboats here and it's nice and smooth. The wind is puffy though; it could be a real mast-breaker out there today."
>
> Thus reassured, I climbed into the right side of the Arrow's cockpit.
>
> I put on a pair of ski goggles, pulled my wool hat over my ears, and drew my parka hood over my wool hat. *"MMmmmmmmm Mmmmmmmmm Mmmmmmmmmm,"* said Jack. I thought to myself, this is going to be great; I can't even hear what he's saying. And I'm going out in an 80-mile-an-hour iceboat with a guy who will be skirting patches of open water.
>
> Jack climbed in beside me and I eased part of my left ear out of the

wool. If he shouted Mayday I wanted to be the first to know. The boat started to move.

"Lean way back," he said, settling himself in a comfortable position and swinging a large wooden tiller to the left. The boat started to move in a graceful arc, to the right. "Some boats steer by foot pedals, and the larger Skeeters have a horizontal wheel under the deck," he said. "Keep your head down."

The boom swung across over my head, there was a snap of canvas.

From the skatelike runners, one on each side on sort of outriggers and a third in front used for steering, there came a hissing sound.

Suddenly, we were going very fast.

"We're just idling now, about 15–20 miles an hour, 'til we get out of the cove," said Jack, doing things with the tiller. It crossed my mind that if this was idling, I would shortly be in some very serious trouble.

I had brought my camera along to take pictures of the boat underway. The camera was under my knees. It suddenly became clear to me that I wasn't going to take any pictures because I would be too busy holding on.

The boat came out of the cove and headed down the vast frozen lake. Vast partly frozen lake, I remembered. Suddenly, it seemed like a giant hand grabbed the boat and shoved it skimming across the ice. The acceleration was breathtaking. Later, Jack said we have reached "maybe a little over 60" but when you're that close to the surface it seems like much, much faster. Tiny pieces of ice dashed against the lower part of my face. Now I knew why everybody wore full face masks.

I considered releasing my two-handed grip on the boat and putting one glove over my face. The boat whipped around and headed in another direction and I decided to hold on, and let my teeth bleed. "Here comes a pressure ridge!" Jack shouted. I didn't know what I was supposed to do about it. Praying seemed appropriate.

We sped up on a long crack, and crossed it *hsssss,* crump, *hsssss.* The crack was just a bump. We tacked back and forth. Suddenly, the wind slowed.

"It's very puffy, and we'll probably have some runners up in the air today." He explained that sailing on just two of the three runners was exciting, but that "if it lifts up too high and then comes down with a bang you lose speed. There are ways to take advantage of the angle, though and WHOOPS there are waves ahead!"

Waves meant open water right in front of us, and before I could even react to the information—like screaming or something—Jack had swung the tiller around and we were speeding back toward the cove.

"Gotta watch out for those places," he said, easily the understatement of the winter.

Maneuvering the boat up near the others in a series of deft tiller movements and adjustments of the main sheet (the rope that controls the sail's angle), Jack brought the iceboat to a stop without even using the brake.

I climbed out of *Skidoo;* I didn't know how to thank him. For one thing, my lips were frozen shut.

Jack understood, and took me back to his car. There, as I warmed up, he told me some more about iceboating. Like the fact that the best Skeeters can go four times the speed of the wind. A race at 70 mph is not uncommon. All sailboats obtain "lift" by sailing at an angle to the wind and this, plus the low surface resistance of the runners makes them go much faster than the actual wind.

He also noted that unlike sailboat races, iceboats tack, or make a zig-zag course, downwind as well as upwind. In an iceboat race, the boats sail back and forth in a series of graceful curves at high speeds.

"From a distance you can't tell who's ahead." Jack added that most sailboat skippers can easily maneuver an iceboat upwind, but that "tacking downwind is what counts and that's the hard part."

I asked him how much the boats cost, and he said they ranged from about $850 for a little DN to about $3,000 for one of the big Skeeters. The heaviest boats there that day were the Yankees, 2-place craft weighing roughly 450 pounds. Members of the iceboating fraternity take them around to different lakes, and to frozen-over shore spots, on the tops of cars, and on trailers.

Just before the group left for their race two miles down to the lake, I talked to another skipper. The wind had picked up. Boats seemed to be flying across the lake, keeping clear, naturally, of those areas marked with Christmas trees.

He looked a little worried, and to me, it was obvious why. But I was wrong again.

"A puffy day like this; it's rough on the boats. You can damage them." As later events proved, the veteran iceboating skippers knew what they were talking about. A short time later, mast-breaking 40-mile gusts hit the reservoir. Two masts were broken, one on a big Skeeter and the other on a Yankee. All races had to be cancelled for the day.

One by one they came in, and the skippers, their wives, and their children helped disassemble them.

Oddly enough, nobody seemed disappointed. A lot of sailing time had been logged, (even the two boats with broken masts were back on the lake Sunday with replacements) and a family-picnic atmosphere had prevailed throughout the weekend.

If this still appeals to you, dear reader, please read on.

Sailing on Ice

1
History

The traditional beginning of iceboating is placed in Holland in the middle 1600s. The original iceboats, we're told, were sailboats fitted with runners and used for moving cargo around the bays and canals adjacent to the North Sea (see figure 1).

Figure 1. Dutch iceboat in the year 1605.

It is well established that by the late 1800s descendents of the Dutch settlers along the Hudson River north of New York built large, stern-steering iceboats for sport. This type is still known as the Hudson River type (see figure 2). The hulls of these craft varied from 30 to as much as 60 feet in length. The largest carried as much as 1,000 square feet of sail area in a mainsail plus a jib. Large basketlike cockpits on either side of the main hull beam lined with thick cushions carried 16 or more passengers. Speeds of 60 mph and more are claimed for these big boats. The sport spread along the northern Atlantic seaboard and then moved west to Michigan and Minnesota where winter ice conditions and wind were excellent on the lakes and rivers.

A major breakthrough in design and performance came in 1933 when Walter Beauvois at William Bay, Wisconsin, built a 13-foot hull with the steering runner in front, a 9-foot runner plank, and only a single, stiffly battened sail of about 75 square feet. He called it the *Beau-skeeter*. It outraced all of the much larger stern steerers that carried up to 10 times the sail area. It was less expensive to build and much easier to transport and assemble.

Figure 2. (a) Hudson River type stern steerer; (b) old stern steerer acting young.

a

b

From it, in subsequent years, the E-class skeeter was developed (see figure 3) which has kept a 75-square-foot sail area limitation. The continuous refinements of this active racing class have made it the fastest of all iceboats up to this writing.

Figure 3. **Typical Skeeter.**

In the middle and late 1930s the Palmer Boat Co. introduced the first factory-built stock boat, an 18-foot-long Skeeter with a 12-foot plank. Competition in building came when Ted Mead in 1938 produced a stock Skeeter of larger dimensions. Both of these seated 2, with side-by-side seating.

The Yankee class iceboat (see figure 4) is a one-design Skeeter first introduced in the East by Ray Ruge, Homer Sieder, and Willi Schmitz in 1946. Its two-place, side-by-side cockpit lends itself to doubles racing as well as singles.

Figure 4. Yankee, one-design Skeeter.

The DN iceboat (see figure 5) is a one-design class developed by Archie Aarel, Joseph Lodge, and Norman Garrett and introduced by the *Detroit News* in 1937 to stimulate interest in the sport (and presumably sell more newspapers). It is a minimum-sized (12-foot) hull, which some say the skipper "wears" rather than rides in. It has a runner plank about 8 feet long. It carries a 60-square-foot sail which is very large for such a small hull. Because the DN is economical to build or buy and can be transported by car roof or in a station wagon, it has become the most popular racing design.

Figure 5. DN, one-design iceboat.

In 1965 the Arrow class boat (see figure 6) was introduced as a "family" boat and designed as a low-maintenance, two-place side-by-side, racing craft. Its fiberglass hull, aluminum spars, and simple strong rigging make it a boat to sail in and not to work on. The Viking, Renegade and Nite classes are similar in sail size and weight, but have springboards. A simple design, using the sail from the sunfish "soft water" sailboat, or another simple design, the Wisp, are very good to introduce the younger set to this exciting sport.

An unorthodox design that performed well is shown in figure 9. A very special type of iceboat, the Scooter was designed originally in the 1930s for the unpredictable salt water ice on the south-shore bays of Long Island, New York. The hull is a watertight boat closely resembling the duck hunting boats of the era. On the bottom are four, almost-full-length runners. The mast is short and carries a mainsail and a large jib. There is no steering runner. Direction relative to the wind is controlled by tightening or loosening the jib. The real advantage of the scooter shows up when the ice under it breaks or it must cross a stretch of water—it floats! It can actually skim across small stretches of water at high speed and can float indefinitely in the water with passengers. With sufficient wind, it can climb

Figure 6. Arrow, one-design iceboat.

Figure 7.
All one design.

a Viking

a Renegade

a Nite

Figure 8. Sunfish sail iceboat.

Figure 9. Stern-steering Skeeter.

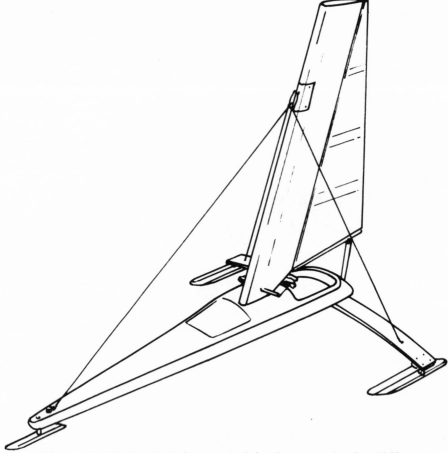

Figure 10. **Rigid-sail iceboat—raced in Germany in the 1960s.**

back on the ice. Learning to control direction with the jib is a challenge; and negotiating a racing course is very tricky. Upsets are frequent but rarely serious to the boat or its occupants.

An example of a rigid airfoil iceboat, one of many types that have been built and tested, is shown in figure 10. In this, a symmetrical airfoil is used in the manner of a very deep mast with a small sail area aft to add area for starting up. Other rigid-sail designs have been built with only a rigid sail. One of these had the skipper's seat actually inside the airfoil. To date, these craft have shown satisfactory speed under controlled wind conditions, but have not shown adequate versatility in all winds and directions to do well in racing.

2
About Iceboats

GENERAL DESCRIPTION

An iceboat is a rather special piece of sporting equipment. It must be extremely strong to withstand the forces of the wind and ice at terrifying speeds. Yet it must be capable of being quickly assembled and disassembled with bare hands in subfreezing weather. It's literally held together by safety pins. Its sail is not at all like that of a sailboat, it is more akin to an airplane wing on edge. It goes faster while tacking into the wind than it does with the wind. It provides the hottest competition under the coldest imaginable conditions for its skipper. To learn more about this strange creature, let's examine it part by part. For the names of the parts, see figure 11.

THE HULL

The hull of an iceboat is sometimes called a fuselage. It does indeed resemble in construction and function the fuselage of a small airplane. It is a streamlined body on which is attached the steering runner (or springboard), the runner plank, and the mast. It also contains the cockpit for the skipper (and passenger).

What does not appear at first glance is that the hull must function as a very, very strong beam. It is not just the weight of the mast and sail that lean down on the mast step on the hull, it is also the

PRINCIPLE PARTS OF AN ICEBOAT

DIMENSIONS OF ONE DESIGN ICEBOATS

TYPE	A	B	C	D	E
ARROW	18	12	11	67	250
DN	16	8	?	60	125
RENEGADE	18.25	16	18	67	300
YANKEE	24	18	NOT SPEC.	75	450
VIKING	18	11.5	14.5	66.5	250

A - MAST LENGTH (FT.)
B - RUNNER PLANK LENGTH (FT.)
C - RUNNER SPACING (FT.)
D - SAIL AREA (SQ. FT.)
E - APPROX. WEIGHT (LBS.)

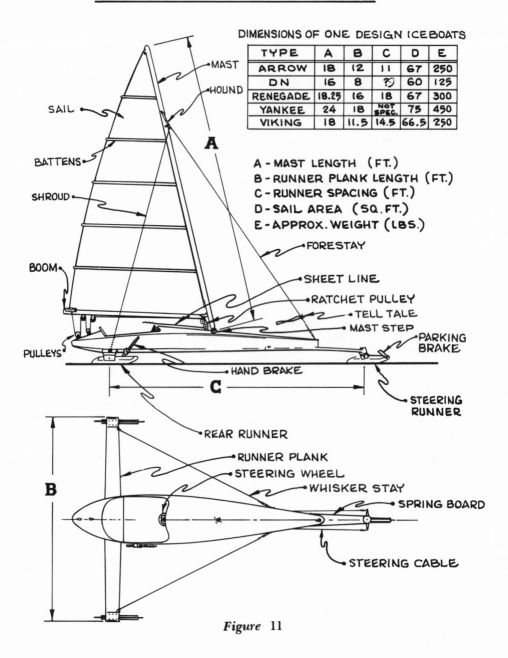

Figure 11

downward pull of the forestay and shroud plus pull on each of the vertical passes of the sheet between the boom and the pulleys in the back of the fuselage.

For this reason the hull must resist bending and breaking in the same sense as a bridge or an I beam does. Wood planks for the sides and bulkheads and plywood for the bottom and deck are commonly used fastened with screws, glue, and metal fittings.

Fiberglass hulls, such as used on the Arrow, are generally reinforced in critical inside areas by wood. Steel tubing with fabric covering, as used on light aircraft, can make an extremely strong, light hull. In any design, thought must be given to the attachment points of the plank, springboard, or steerer, tiller or wheel, handbrake, deck pulleys, forestay, and the back-breaking mast-step fixture.

The cockpit is made no larger than necessary for the one or more occupants. Because the natural shape of the hull is long and narrow, streamlining is easily accomplished. Cross-sectional area should not be made larger for sake of looks or for added room inside because streamlining is too important for good performance.

THE RUNNER PLANK

The runner plank is one of the hardest working parts of the iceboat. Varying in length from 8 feet on a DN to 18 feet plus on Skeeters, the plank is usually made of two or more wood laminations glued together. It is formed into a convex upward arc so that under full load it bends to an approximately flat shape. Sitka spruce has been favored wood for planks because of its strength and light weight. It is reasonable to assume that other materials such as tempered steel tubing, reinforced fiberglass, or other flexible structures could serve as runner planks, but to date nothing threatens to replace wood.

For best strength to weight, and to distribute the bending over the whole plank, it is usually tapered either in thickness or in planform, or both. Bolt holes for holding the plank to the hull should be as small as possible since they weaken it in the area of greatest bending moment. At the ends where the runner chocks are fastened, extra thickness is allowed to prevent splitting. In larger iceboats cables called "whisker stays" keep the runner plank at right angles to the hull. The plank should be protected from being marred by the skipper's shoe cleats by step pads near the hull. It should be kept covered with a good varnish or paint so that water cannot get between the laminations and unglue them. To help the plank maintain its shape during the summer, store the runner so that the bend is supported in the middle.

On the ice try to be easy on the plank by coming off a hike gently and not overloading your boat. A hard jibe when moving slowly in high wind will cause the shroud to snap tight. If the shroud does not break, the plank can. Snubbers on the shroud are used on some craft to help reduce the shock in this case.

The flexibility of a runner plank affects the handling speed. Most racing enthusiasts find that a more flexible plank is preferable to a stiffer one. Of course, it cannot be so flexible that it breaks or sags to the ice in the center under strong wind conditions or heavy passenger loads.

THE SPRINGBOARD

The three- to five-foot, flexible member mounted on the front of some hulls and carrying the steering runner is called a springboard. The first front steerers did not have springboards. DN and Arrows don't have them now. One might well ask why a springboard is needed. Why not just build a longer hull, if one wants a longer wheelbase between the plank and steerer? The answer is that the springboard does much more than lengthen the hull.

First, the hull must be rigid to withstand the bending forces occasioned by the downward push of the mast and the upward pull of the forestay and sheet lines. The springboard, being in front of the forestay does not need to be so strong as the hull. It can be flexible and act as a long, soft spring. This not only gives a larger triangular platform between the three runners for stability, but it acts as a shock absorber for the front. When the steering runner on a hull without a springboard hits a bump, not only the front of the hull bounces up, but the mast and sail are forced to tip quickly backward. This shakes the sail and makes it temporarily lose its shape and hence its driving force. So it loses speed. With a springboard, only the runner and free end of the springboard move up and down quickly on bumps. The inertia of the rest of the craft keeps it steady.

On a turn, if a rigid front runner hits a bump, it lifts off the ice. This allows it to move sideways in the air. This means loss of positive steering control. Worse, when the runner comes back on the ice it is skidding. This causes a speed loss that can be avoided with a springboard. It keeps the steerer pressed to the ice even when there are bumps. Of course, the springboard adds greatly to riding comfort and to the longevity of other parts of the boat which are then protected from riding shocks. It also reduces the sensitivity of the steering, giving a feeling of greater stability in holding a heading.

A hull must be designed to take the extra bending moment on it caused by long leverage of the springboard. In addition, adding a springboard to an existing iceboat takes weight off the front runner and adds it to the runner plank. This causes extra load on the plank which causes it to bend lower in the center.

When a conversion to a springboard is made, the extra load on the hull can be avoided by making the springboard pivot at the bow of the hull and then extend all the way back to and attach to the runner plank. Of course this means some extra weight.

In summary, a springboard, when properly designed to the iceboat, adds to its performance in many ways, particularly on rough ice with good wind. The springboard does add weight and possibly wind resistance to a hull and hence may prove to be a slight detriment to performance in light air with smooth ice.

THE CHOCKS

In an iceboat, the device on which the runner is mounted is called a chock. There are two types in wide usage—the channel-and-bolt type, as shown in figure 12, and the more elaborate shaft-and-

Figure 12. Rear runner in chock, DN and Arrow.

pillow block type shown in figures 13 and 14. In both types the object is to allow the runner to pivot easily about a horizontal, athwartship axis without any side play about any other axis. The two chocks on the runner plank should have an adjustment capability to assure perfect fore and aft alignment (see section on alignment).

The steering chock is mounted on an approximately vertical axis for turning. For increased stability, the axis may lean backwards as does the fork on a bicycle. The rear chocks may also have adjustments or fixed wedge angles to assure that the runners stand perpendicular to the ice when the boat is loaded. With a square-set chock, the tops of the runners may lean outward due to the curvature of the plank. This causes a small amount of extra runner drag and may cause the runner to slip sideways when hiking.

Most skippers prefer that the runners be very free to pivot in the chocks, but should have no side play. Others claim that a little side play is good in light wind because it permits runners, which are not perfectly aligned, to align themselves and hence reduce drag.

Figure 13. (a) **Pillow-block chock on Skeeter; (b) angle-iron runner.**

a

b

STEERING MECHANISMS

There are several methods used for control of the steering runner. No one method has proven superior to the others enough to replace them; it is largely a matter of preference.

The simplest steering is on the stern-steerer boat. In these, a shaft on the steering runner pivot is directly connected to a tiller that is operated by hand. It is hinged vertically to facilitate getting under it and to prevent strain on the tiller itself should it be pushed upward or downward inadvertently.

The DN and Arrow class boats, employ a triangular wooden tiller mounted on a rotatable vertical shaft extending from the deck through the hull. Beneath the hull on the shaft is a cross arm that drives a similar cross arm on the steering runner by rods or by two parallel cables with pin and clevis joints on each end. The tiller may be used to steer by hand or may be held between the sailor's knees, and the steering accomplished by moving one's bent knees from side to side. This frees both hands for working the sheet. These tillers are hinged to move vertically for access to the cockpit and strain relief. This arrangement makes it possible to bend the sheet over the handle of the tiller to relieve the strain on the arms in heavy wind.

PILLOW BLOCK CHOCK
(USED ON LARGER ICE BOATS)

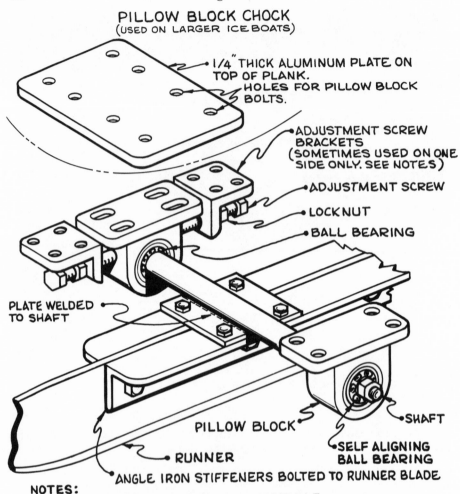

• 1/4" THICK ALUMINUM PLATE ON TOP OF PLANK.
• HOLES FOR PILLOW BLOCK BOLTS.

• ADJUSTMENT SCREW BRACKETS (SOMETIMES USED ON ONE SIDE ONLY. SEE NOTES)

• ADJUSTMENT SCREW

• LOCK NUT

• BALL BEARING

PLATE WELDED TO SHAFT

PILLOW BLOCK •

• SHAFT

• RUNNER

• SELF ALIGNING BALL BEARING

• ANGLE IRON STIFFENERS BOLTED TO RUNNER BLADE

NOTES:
1 - ONLY ONE PILLOW BLOCK IS ADJUSTABLE.
2 - PILLOW BLOCKS AND SCREW BRACKETS ARE BOLTED THROUGH BODY FIT HOLES IN RUNNER PLANK.
3 - BOLTS IN PILLOW BLOCKS ARE LOOSENED WHEN ADJUSTMENT IS MADE.

Figure 14

In the partially enclosed cockpit iceboats such as the Skeeters and Yankees either wheel or foot-pedal steering, or even both, are used.

The foot pedals linked to a bar mounted on a vertical axis rotate it through a limited angle. The ends of this bar are connected to a similar crosswise bar on the steering runner by cables. Cables can be parallel to steer, like a sled, or can be crossed to steer to the side on which the pedal is depressed, as in an airplane. Foot steer-

Figure 15. Steering runner, DN.

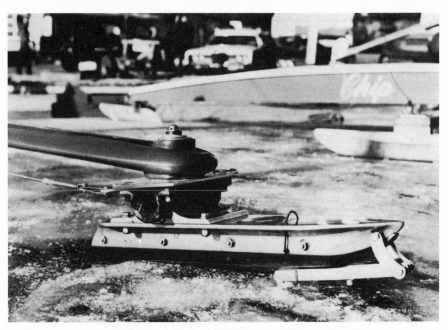

Figure 16. Steering runner, Skeeter.

ing has the advantage of leaving both hands free to work the sheet. Its main disadvantage is the lack of control during the pushing at the start. Not until the sailor has climbed aboard and gotten properly seated, can he control his direction. For this reason foot-steerer boats sometimes have in addition a small hand wheel for steering at the start. In a side-by-side seating arrangment as in a Yankee, if the pedals are placed centrally for single occupancy, they are difficult to use when two people are in the boat.

For this reason, the wheel is used, sometimes as the only means of steering, and sometimes in addition to the foot pedals. For ease in access, the 10- to 12-inch diameter steering wheel is generally mounted on a stud fixed to the underside of the deck above the sailor's lap. The steering cables are wound around a drum on the wheel, pass through suitable guides and pulleys, to the steering runner cross bar. Where both wheel and pedals are used, they work in parallel. Instead of the cable and drum on the wheel, a sprocket and a piece of bicycle chain can be used. Ends of the chain are attached by cable to the steering runner and pedals. The steering runner itself is mounted as shown in figure 18.

Figure 17. Cockpit of Skeeter.

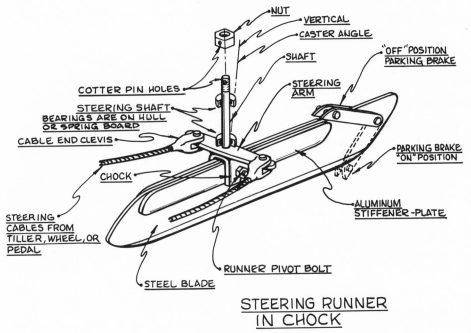

NUT
VERTICAL
CASTER ANGLE
SHAFT
"OFF" POSITION PARKING BRAKE
COTTER PIN HOLES
STEERING ARM
STEERING SHAFT
BEARINGS ARE ON HULL OR SPRING BOARD
CABLE END CLEVIS
PARKING BRAKE "ON" POSITION
CHOCK
STEERING CABLES FROM TILLER, WHEEL, OR PEDAL
ALUMINUM STIFFENER-PLATE
STEEL BLADE
RUNNER PIVOT BOLT

STEERING RUNNER IN CHOCK

Figure 18

The runner pivots on its horizontal axis the same as the larger ones on the runner plank. The chock is mounted on the steering shaft, which carries the steering bar. This shaft may be vertical, but there is an advantage to having it lean backwards 10° to 15°. This backward lean angle so-called caster angle. The advantage of caster is that it makes the weight of the boat try to keep the runner aiming straight ahead. Thus, it gives an iceboat directional stability. It is desirable to have low friction in the steering shaft as well as the rest of the steering mechanism so that the caster can do its job of keeping the boat straight and the steering smooth.

Backlash or springiness in the steering system is very undesirable. It causes lack of precise control and permits unevenness in the ice to divert the steering runner, taking the control away from the skipper. Breaking a steering cable can cause a very serious accident in two ways: with loss of control you may strike another iceboat, obstruction, or a spectator, or the runner, being pulled by one cable, may turn sideways and cause your craft to upset. One must be very sure the cables and fittings are sound and that any pulleys on the steering cables are firmly fastened to the hull. Check cable for wear or fraying at pulleys and rubbing areas. Be careful that the sheet line does not catch in any of the steering pulleys or sprockets.

BRAKES

The Hand Brake

A hand brake is usually a hand-operated lever pivoted on the runner plank or the side of the hull. It can also be mounted on the hull centerline forward of the mast and protrude through the bottom when actuated by cable from a knob or lever in the cockpit. Its lower end has one or more sharp points that can be forced against the ice (see figure 4). A hand brake at best is a very ineffective means of stopping an iceboat traveling at more than a few knots. However, after you have come up into the wind and are nearly stopped, it can be a great boat saver—yours and those already parked. Many regattas require a hand brake on every boat as a protection for the parked boats and yourself. Remember, don't count on it to do any good at high speed. A really good skipper uses it very little in stopping. In racing, a hand brake is useful to hold the boat on the line before the starting flag is dropped.

The Parking Brake

This brake is attached to the front runner and is used when the boat is not occupied (see figure 18). The points that dig into the ice should be kept sharp. The bolt through the runner should be tight enough to create friction so that the brake won't bounce forward while sailing. This could cause an upset, so be sure it is folded all the way back before starting.

THE SAIL AND MAST

Modern high-performance iceboats have a single sail. Jibs are used on the venerable, Hudson River type stern steerers to balance the forces out and help steering, and on Scooters as a means for steering. A correctly proportioned bow steerer needs no jib. In fact, it is in no way improved by adding a jib.

The design of iceboats for high performance has shown that there is a maximum practical sail area for any given-sized triangle formed by the three runners. To go larger in area might help slightly in light wind, but would be a detriment in heavy wind. For a given length of hull, the sail area is usually about a third that of a water sailboat. The difference is accounted for by the fact that the iceboat with its low runner resistance and high speed uses its sail more like the wing of an airplane, knifing at a small angle to the relative wind. A sailboat running before the wind uses it more like a parachute. Because of its high drag hull and low relative wind speed, the sailboat needs more area when tacking. While streamlining the mast and rigging help a sailboat to gain up to 10 percent in speed, in an iceboat the effect of good streamlining could almost double the speed.

An iceboat mast is made of wood (usually spruce) or streamlined aluminum alloy tubing. The wood mast can be made tapered both in thickness and depth. To increase the effective sail area, the fore and aft dimension at the cross section is made to measure as much as 10 inches. It is carefully streamlined and the wood is varnished and sanded for a perfectly smooth surface to cut wind drag. The mast is mounted on the bottom on a ball joint which permits it to pivot fore and aft, athwartship, and also to rotate in direction.

MAST AND SAIL PARTS

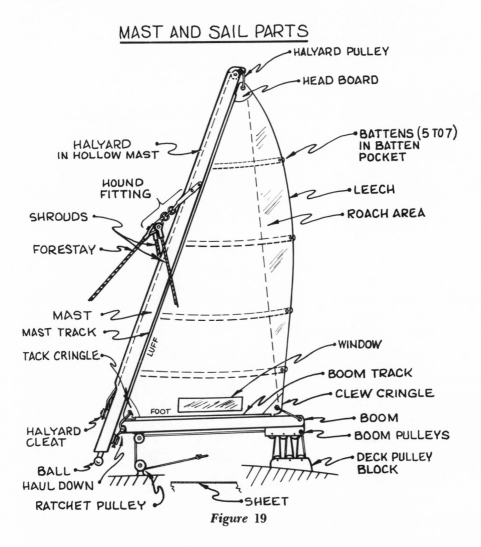

Figure 19

About two-thirds of the way up, it is supported by a fitting on the mast (known as a hound). This fitting connects by a flexible linkage or chain to a triangular plate to which is fastened the upper ends of the two shrouds going to the ends of the runner plank and the forestay (or bowstay) going to the front of the hull (see figures 20 and 21). There is a tubular track in the trailing edge of the mast which accepts the luff rope from the sail. Because the mast is free to swivel, the streamlined mast automatically aligns itself with the sail when there is wind in the sail.

The forward boom end is pivotally fastened to the mast in a fitting that is in a track permitting it to move up and down the mast. To tighten the luff of the sail, this fitting can be pulled downward and on some rigs, locked.

The boom is oval or flat in cross section and carries a track in its upper surface into which the sail's foot rope slides. As in the mast there is provision to stretch the foot rope and clamp or tie it. It is generally stretched more tightly for high wind conditions than for light wind.

The halyard is usually passed through a curved tube, or over a pulley, at the masthead and either lies outside on the leading edge

Figure 20. Hound fitting, Skeeter.

Figure 21. Hound fitting, DN and Arrow.

of the mast, or better, comes down the inside of the hollow mast and is cleated where it emerges from a hole in the mast, near the deck. The halyard is in the form of a steel cable from the sail to the cleat. It has a detachable rope section attached by a snap hook when the sail is down and taken off when the sail is raised. Sails may have a window of flexible, transparent plastic along the foot permitting the skipper to see to leeward when the boom is hauled down close to the deck.

Iceboat sails have 4 to 7 full-length wood or fiberglass battens to stiffen the sail. The sail material was formerly a tight woven cotton. This has been replaced in modern sails by a synthetic textile (Dacron is good) of 6 to 12½ ounces per square-foot weight. It is advantageous for a sail to have a high ratio of height to area. This is so that for a given sail area the greatest volume of passing air will be deflected. Since the wind usually increases in velocity with altitude above the ice, the higher sail will reach into the higher velocity wind and give more driving force and speed. Because an ice sail always works at a small angle to the wind (angle of attack) it is unnecessary to have much length along the boom; in fact more length here means more drag and is undesirable at high speeds. It helps, however, in getting underway in light wind. The shape of the sail would ideally be that of an airplane wing. The sails of highly refined skeeters with very deep, thin, streamlined masts and short booms approach this ideal very closely. The sail on Skeeters is kept tight along its mast, by a downhaul fitting, or cable, which stretches the sail downward after the sail has been raised to the masthead and cleated.

Even without a downhaul, the sheet line that goes through two pulleys near the foot of the mast on an Arrow or DN accomplished the downhaul function while the multiple pulleys at the rear of the boom keep the leech tightly stretched (see figure 22).

Figure 22. Boom and pulleys.

The amount of pocket, or concavity of the sail is a compromise. A deep pocket provides good acceleration and light wind performance, while a flatter sail usually gives a higher top speed. All ice sails tend to be much flatter than those of sailboats.

The sail is flattened by the force of sheet and pulleys stretching the leech and bending the top of the mast backward when it is sheeted in. Tremendous forces can be built up by hard sheeting in. The forestay and hull must be strong enough to accommodate these forces. If the sail has the proper pocket, shape, battens, and elasticity, it will vary in concavity from the good pocket for starting and light wind when sheeted loosely, to a flatter airfoil shape when sheeted in hard for high speed.

To gain extra effective sail area under the 75 square feet rule for Skeeters, there are three means commonly used. First, the fore and aft depth of the mast is made as much as 10 inches. This also improves streamlining. Second, the boom is made deep and thin so that it actually adds 8 to 10 inches to the height of the sail. Third, the roach of the sail is made as large as can be controlled by battens within the 12 inch limitation set forth in the rules (see appendix on Skeeter rules). This permits an extra sail area of up to 25 square feet to be attained with a 75-square-foot sail measured in accordance with the rules.

Battens

Battens are flat strips of wood or fiberglass that are slipped into long thin pockets in a sail to give it shape and a degree of rigidity. The roach of the sail (which is outside the triangle formed by the mast and boom) could not be held in shape at all without battens. The batten pockets are usually sewn into the sail parallel to the seams. This makes them nearly perpendicular to the leech on most sails. The pocket is bottomed just short of the luff rope so they do not tend to jamb the sail in the channel of the mast when the sail is raised or lowered. Wood (ash or hickory) is the traditional batten material, but fiberglass and other plastics are gaining in popularity. Typical batten dimensions on modern sails are about $\frac{1}{4}$ inch by 2 inches wide and a length depending on sail dimensions. One or more holes in the aft end of the batten permit the batten to be fastened to grommets in the leech of the sail by "lift-the-dot" snap fasteners, short pieces of cord, or other fastener (see figure 23). There is a diversity of opinion on how flexible (thin) the batten should be; also on whether they should be of constant thickness or vary in thickness in a special way along their length. One theory held by the variable thickness advocates is that the batten should be thinner over the forward one-quarter to one-third of its length so that under wind pressure it forms an airfoil curvature. Others rely on the wind pressure itself to form the "perfect" airfoil using thin, constant thickness battens. Of course the batten cannot be too thin or it will break, or too flexible or it will not perform its function.

Another variable in the use of battens is on how tight they

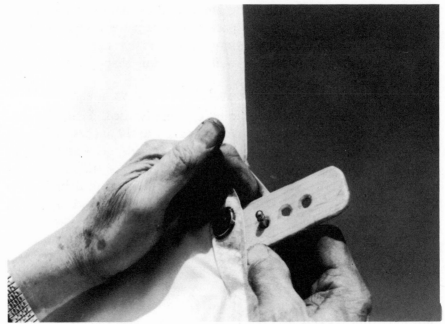

Figure **23. Batten with snap fastener.**

stretch the sail parallel to the pocket. If a more forward hole in the batten is used for fastening it to the sail, it will just lie loosely in the pocket. However, if the batten is pushed into the pocket so it presses on the pocket bottom, the sail is stretched. For this a hole nearer the end of the batten is used. The batten will be under compression and the sail under tension parallel to the batten. This latter method forces the sail to form a curvature. It is alleged that this curvature has the benefit of holding a good airfoil shape in a wind too light to form a good shape by wind pressure alone. This effect is exaggerated by using thinner battens and, of course, varied by using battens of nonuniform thickness. Any advantage gained by optimizing battens can be important to iceboat performance. Some sailors have two or more sets of battens available to be used depending on wind conditions and as spares in case of breakage during a regatta.

Mast Rake

In all modern iceboats the mast leans backward to some extent. This angle to the vertical is called *rake*. Where class rules permit it, the rake is adjustable both by changing the length of the forestay and by moving the fixture for the mast fore and aft on the hull.

A benefit of rake is that it permits the leech of the sail to be shortened for a given area. This means the shape of the sail is more under control by the mast and boom and can be made to more closely approximate the ideal airfoil section. There are other, often conflicting, claims made for increasing rake. Apart from the fact that it gives the craft a look of speed, even when standing still, most of the benefits of extreme rake have yet to be proven. One bad effect of rake is that it puts extra bending strain on the hull and tension on the forestay. This requires extra weight to strengthen the hull and thicker, less streamlined stays.

DN and Arrow class boats (figures 5 and 6) have a small amount of rake and hence a long leech on the sail. Typical Skeeter sails (figure 3) have sufficient rake to make the leech nearly vertical and as short as possible.

Mast Slop

The mast is supported by the two shrouds from the runner plank ends and the forestay from the bow. These all join at their upper ends on the hound fitting. This fitting is directly above a point that is about a third of the distance from the runner plank to the front of the hull. Hence, no backstay is needed to position the mast.

The shrouds are always left a certain amount loose. This permits the mast an amount of side-to-side freedom which is indelicately referred to as *slop*. Slop is used for several purposes. In some craft it helps the mast to rotate correctly when the windward shroud and the forestay tighten. It also provides room for the sail to swing way out when starting, since the shroud on the lee side is slack.

Where slop is made adjustable by extender fittings on the shrouds, it is often increased on extremely windy days. Increased slop makes the force vector of the wind on the sail aim more downward rather than nearly horizontal. This significantly reduces the tendency for the iceboat to tip (hike) at a small sacrifice to useful thrust due to wind spillage.

As more slop is permitted in the mast, the bending forces on the hull are increased in both the vertical and horizontal sense and also the bending on the plank is greater. The tension on the shrouds is also increased with increased slop and this at a time of strong wind and gusts. So be sure your rig can take it, if you want to experiment with either more rake or more slop in the mast.

Putting elastic snubbers on the shrouds is helpful. These take up the slack in the leeward shroud and alleviate the peak tension on the shroud caused by gusts while tacking or when a jibe is made at very low boat speed and the mast snaps the shroud tight. When the shroud tightens, the snubber is stretched and takes up some of the shock. An automobile shock absorber, a screen-door closer or a piece of inner tube can be used for this purpose.

ABOUT RUNNERS

The importance of having correctly shaped runners and keeping them sharpened at all times cannot be overemphasized. There is no simple machine that will do the original shaping or the subsequent sharpening correctly. It takes skill, patience, and a thorough knowledge of how a runner operates on the ice to make or resharpen them.

It is an interesting fact that the runner does not slide on the ice. The pressure built up by the weight of the iceboat on the fine runner edge is enough to melt a groove in the ice. Thus, the runner is separated from the ice by a lubricating film of water. This is why it slides so easily. In extremely cold weather, the water does not form and the friction of runner on ice is higher. Furthermore, since it cannot melt a groove in the ice, the runner does not resist side slip so well. The colder the weather, the sharper must be your runners. The sharper runner has a higher unit presssure on the ice, which helps the melting. When extremely sharp runners are used on ice that is near melting temperature, they dig in unnecessarily deep and cause more friction than slightly duller runners. In this "warmer" ice, the dull runner will dig in sufficiently to prevent side slip.

Now, let's look in detail at the part of the runner that touches the ice (see figure 24). It is made out of steel plate one-fourth to one-half inch thick depending on the size and weight of the iceboat. Unlike a skate, an iceboat runner has a V bottom. The angle of the V is about 80°. It may vary from 75° to 90° depending upon the manufacturer and the type of ice it is to be used on. Harder ice can use a smaller angle.

Other things being equal, the iceboat rides smoother and holds the turns better the lighter the weight of the runners and chocks. Looking at the runner from the side, it is flat only for about one-sixth of its length. This section is located under the pivot point which is usually located from 33 to 40 percent of the runner length from the heel. From this flat section, the sharpened edge is curved up (rockered) toward the toe and the heel in a very large radius. The last two inches or so of the running edge is not sharp but is

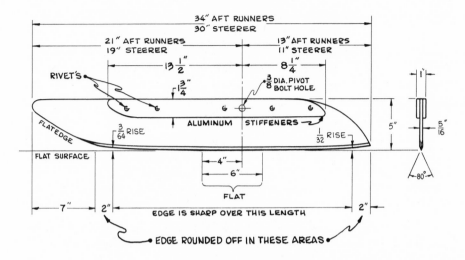

TYPICAL RUNNER
(DIMENSION ARE FOR ARROW. DN IS SAME, BUT SHORTER)

Figure **24**

rounded off at both the foreward and aft ends. The sharply curved up part of the runner in front is not sharpened at all. It usually has a flat bottom with the corners rounded off. The heel is very slightly rounded for safety in handling. The flat section under the pivot gets a firm hold on the ice and makes the runner want to go straight. If it is too long, the blade will not dig into the ice deeply enough and also it will be too difficult to turn when steering. The sections just fore and aft of the flat section, which are slightly curved, give more length actually embedded in the ice when it gets softer. Also they let the runner move smoothly over small irregularities on the ice surface.

The big turnup in front makes the runner climb over large bumps, ridges, or sticks in the ice up to about 4 inches high. On smooth ice this front serves no purpose. Even apparently perfectly smooth ice usually has, from place to place, many little bumps of one-eighth inch or less. As the front of the blade hits these bumps, it first pushes up the rounded-off part of the sharpened length. If the whole blade were flat, this would cause the tip of the heel to dig in.

With the small amount of rocker, the blade merely rocks back a little. The heel, being rounded on the bottom, does not dig in but slides smoothly. This provides the least amount of cracking of the ice for low friction and also keeps a reasonable length of sharpened edge on the ice to prevent side slip.

Most runners are made of cold-rolled steel because of price and machinability. On clean ice they remain sharp for a dozen hours of sailing. However, dust, sand, shells left by birds, stones, cans, bottles, fishhooks, and many unexpected things on the ice will dull the runners in a very short time. To make the edge last longer, some blades are of hardened steel, either the whole blade or just the bottom edge, may be hardened. A hardened blade will take dust, shells, and cans without dulling appreciably. However, glass and stones will still ruin the edge. On the bad side, the hardened blade is more difficult to sharpen. Stainless-steel ones, while expensive, have the advantage of not rusting while stored.

Stiffeners are used on flat steel blades to prevent them from bending—they may be of aluminum or steel. Flat side plates as shown in figure 12 are used for runners in simple chocks in the Arrow and DN boats.

Stiffeners made of steel or aluminum angle give a much more rigid runner and one that will not let the runner bend if it should catch in shell ice (see figure 13). Angle stiffeners must be high enough off the ice so they do not drag on snow patches because this causes severe speed loss. Angle stiffeners are often bent to curve up like a ski in front in order to make the runner climb up on snow patches. These angle stiffeners can save a runner from cutting completely through thin ice in some situations.

SHARPENING RUNNERS

The most important consideration when sharpening a runner is to have the V angle and the rocker of the blade. A runner may be sharpened using a 10- to 12-inch long flat single cut, mill file or a power belt sander using 80 grit for first grind and 120 grit for the finishing. Always file lengthwise on the blade and take only a little at a time. It is advisable to use some kind of a fixture to keep the file or sander at the correct V angle. Figure 25 shows a belt sander with a piece of angle iron attached as a guide for the runner. To keep the rocker shape, you must take the same amount off the edge of the whole blade. Also be careful to take the same off both sides so that the V stays symmetrical and straight in line. After filing or sanding, the edge should be honed lengthwise with a fine oil stone to remove the toolmarks and the burrs on the sharp edge. The rounded-off sections of the edge at the ends should also be made smooth by stoning. For a really fast runner, the edges can be machine buffed with a

Figure 25. Belt sander with angle bracket.

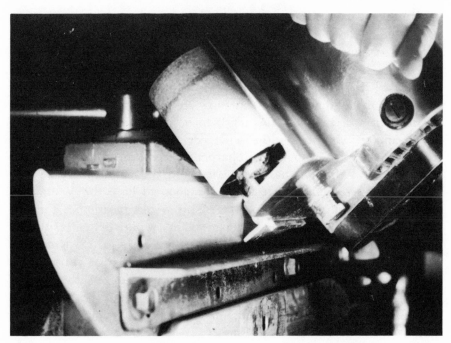

Figure 26. Sharpening runner with belt sander.

cloth wheel and buffing compound to give a mirror finish. This
may sound extreme, but a little bit of difference can win a race.

Should you get a deep nick in the blade, it is not necessary to cut
the whole blade down to the level of the bottom of the nick. Instead,
sharpen the blade ignoring the nick. Next, with a small stone round
the edges of the nick losing as little of the sharp blade edge as possible.

While sharpening, check the blade for any bending sideways. It
can be restraightened using an arbor press or with a heavy hammer
when supported on two blocks. Use thin blocks to prevent overbend-
ing when it is hammered.

Always keep a layer of oil or Vaseline on the blade when not
in use. Rust can severely pit a blade during summer storage, if it is
not protected. The device shown in Figure 27a makes for easy oil-
ing of the runners especially if they are left on and the iceboat is
parked on horses on the ice between sailing days. Foldable horses
can be made simply from two pieces of ½" x 12" x 18" plywood,
a hinge of heavy carpet, and a short piece of rope knotted to keep
the legs at the correct angle (see figure 33) —three are required.
Never leave the iceboat standing on its runners overnight; remove the
runners when you are through for the day. A runner box keeps them
from being nicked and makes them easier to carry or drag across the
ice.

Runners made from pieces of hardened steel angle iron are simple to build, light, and they give a maximum width between runner
edges (see figure 13b). Runners may also be made of wood with
an edge of bent steel angle iron or square stock bolted on. Wooden
runners of this type are usually ½ to ⅞ inches thick, which permits them to be used on soft and snow ice where a thin blade would
cut in. The wood runner also tends to be lighter in weight which is
an advantage. Sharpening the wide edge of these runners is more
difficult than for a thin blade. Sharpening the rear runners with an
asymmetrical V bottom has been tried and successfully used by racing enthusiasts. In theory, it would be good to have the V on each
plank runner aiming to the outside. This would mean that the leeward runner, which has most weight on it, would better resist side
sliding at the expense of a lesser grip by the lightly loaded windward
runner. However, to do this and have the gliding edge run true in
the forward direction, requires a complex shaping of the runner
blade. An extreme example of this would be to grind the blade with
a single cut at say 20° to the horizontal and bend the blade so it will
run true on the rockered portions.

ALIGNING THE PLANK AND RUNNERS

The larger-sized iceboats, such as the Skeeters, have cables called whisker stays running from the ends of the runner plank to the front of the hull. These stays are usually fitted with turnbuckles so they can be adjusted in length. Before aligning the runners, measure the exact distance between the points of attachment of these two whisker stays and adjust the turnbuckles and make them equal. This assures that the runner plank is perpendicular to the centerline of the hull.

In smaller iceboats, such as the Arrow and DN, the plank is firmly bolted to the fuselage and held in alignment by projections on the hull or bolts so no whisker stays are necessary.

If the plank is not aligned, the boat will crab along at an angle. It can best be detected by noting that while going straight, the trace of the steering runner will not be exactly midway between the traces of the two plank runners. This will cause the boat to hike more easily on one side than on the other. It also tends to warp your judgment of the telltale angle and will cause some loss in speed.

In order to have the least sliding resistance, it is essential that the two runners on the runner plank be as close to parallel as possible. For adjusting this parallelism, the chocks that hold the runners should have some means of adjustment. This can be merely a clearance in the bolt holes of a group of bolts that holds the chock to the plank, or a sophisticated jackscrew adjustment that permits an almost micrometer adjustment. Figure 14 shows typical chock attachments. In addition to being parallel, it is desirable to have the runners at right angles to the plank so that the plank travels precisely sideways and does not crab at an angle. This assures that the steering runner tracks in the center of the plank.

When aligning the runners, it is advisable to have the normal sailing weight in the iceboat. This is because as the runner plank bends, it sometimes also twists so that the runner changes from the unloaded position.

Before any measurements are made, you must be certain that there is no angular play of the runner in the chock, and also that the runners are not being forced by the ice into an unnatural toe-in or toe-out position. Tighten the pivot bolts, if you have simple chocks, and push the iceboat ahead and back two or three feet while you bounce up and down on the plank so that the runners come to their natural position on the ice.

The simplest method of measuring for parallelism is to use a steel measuring tape. With a person in the boat for loading, two more people can measure the exact distances between the toes and the heels of the main runners. Measurement should be as accurate as possible because the distances should be the same within 1/32 inch (1mm). To eliminate the need for three people, a measuring device as shown in Figure 27b can be built and used. With this, one person can stand near the hull on the plank and measure the toe and heel distances by himself.

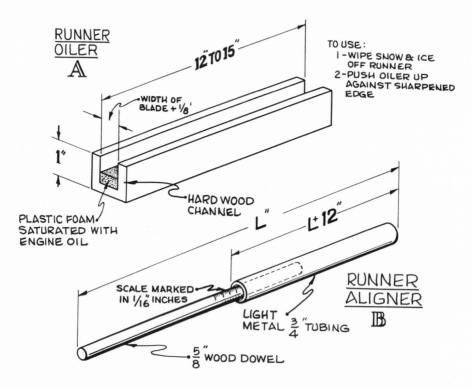

L = DISTANCE BETWEEN RUNNERS ON PLANK
TO USE:
  1- HAVE ICE BOAT ON SMOOTH ICE
  2- HAVE NORMAL SAILING WEIGHT IN BOAT
  3- TIGHTEN RUNNER BOLTS SO NO PLAY EXISTS
  4- PUSH BOAT FORWARD OUT OF PARKING RUTS
  5- EXTEND ALIGNER UNTIL ENDS TOUCH BOTH BLADES AT
     FRONT AND NOTE MEASUREMENT ON SCALE
  6- REPEAT ON HEELS OF BLADE ADJUST CHOCKS TO EQUALIZE
  7- DIFFERENCE SHOULD BE SMALL AS POSSIBLE, NOT OVER
     1/2 DIVISION, OR 1/32 "

Figure 27. Top, runner oiler; *bottom,* runner aligner.

These simple measurement methods check runner parallelism but not perpendicularity to the plank. To do both jobs with precision the alignment fixture shown in figure 28 is used. Each of the runners is set in the pair of V notches of the raised bosses on the plates. Each whole plate is then adjusted back and forth so that the runner pivot axis is directly over a calibration mark on the plate. Next the length of black fishline on one plate is stretched tight, on the pins provided, from one plate to the other. When the runners are both parallel to each other and perpendicular to the centerline between pivot axes, the string will be right along the scribe lines drawn on both plates. If it is out, the amount of misalignment of each chock is quite obvious and proper adjustments should be made.

Figure 28. Runner alignment fixture.

FASTENINGS

An iceboat has a great many little fittings, bolts, and clevises that are needed to hold the various parts together and permit them to be taken apart easily in a cold wind. It is a rule that every connecting device must be locked against opening accidentally by the extreme forces, jolts, and vibrations to which the rig is subjected. The sheet pulleys and the cables used for steering, shrouds, bowstay, and halyard are generally terminated in pin and clevis joints as shown in figure 29. To lock the pin in place, a safety pin is used. So that

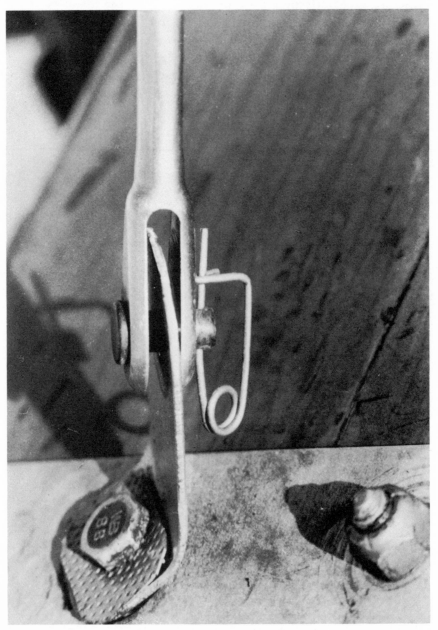

Figure 29. Pin and clevis joint.

the stays can be adjusted in length, extender tubes are used with multiple holes for the clevis pin. These permit the length to be changed in increments determined by the hole spacing. For steering cables, turnbuckles are sometimes used to take up any unwanted slack. The turnbuckle must never be counted on to stay in place by friction, it must be secured with safety wire.

The runner in simple "U" chock is pivoted on a bolt with a nut. This nut should either be of a self-locking type or be secured by a cotter pin through a hole in the threaded end of the bolt.

Bolts on steering wheel, tiller, and steering chock should always have either self-locking nuts, safety pins, or cotter pins to be certain they can never come loose.

Every good iceboater's toolbox has spare safety pins, clevis pins, cotter pins, nuts, and bolts. If you really want to unnerve your competitor in a race, just drop a spare safety pin on the seat in his cockpit when he is lined up for the start. Your sportsmanship may be in question, but imagine the questions in his mind on what's going to fall apart during the race.

STREAMLINING

In the Skeeter class where there are no limitations on design except sail area, attention to streamlining is very important in obtaining a high ratio of boat speed to wind speed.

On good ice with well-sharpened and aligned runners, the runner resistance is only a tiny fraction of the wind resistance at normal sailing speeds. Hence, the ultimate speed for a given sail shape on any heading is almost entirely determined by the wind resistance. Everything on the iceboat contributes to air drag, so every part should be considered for streamlining.

The mast shape is of utmost importance not only to reduce drag, but to assure smooth flow over the sail to get maximum driving force. The cross section should be as long and thin as is consistent with adequate strength. Special attention should be given at the hound fitting to prevent turbulence there. A smooth finish to the mast and even waxing insures low wind resistance. The hull, fortunately, is streamlined by functional design in a bow steerer. For the Skeeter, the cross-sectional area should be kept no bigger than necessary to fit the skipper in a semireclining position. Second cockpit and other openings should be closed when not in use for minimum drag. The aft end is not critical, since the skipper's head and the deck pulleys create turbulence that would negate most efforts to streamline.

A transparent streamlined plastic canopy and a single sheet cable would appear to do a great deal to clean up the back of the hull. However, in a race the effect of the skipper losing the "feel of the wind" might well offset the gain in streamlining. The runner plank creates a great deal of drag because it has a large frontal area and has turbulence-producing intersections with the hull. Widening the plank and giving it a symmetrical airfoil section helps a lot. Some boats use a section with more camber (convexity) on the bottom or ailerons operated by the skipper to create a negative lift to fight a hiking tendency. This does give higher drag, so its net affect is debatable.

Figure 30. Skeeter with streamlined runner plank.

The chocks are another item in which streamlining can play a part. Simple chocks offer less resistance than pillow block types. Bolts and nuts protruding do make a difference, however small. The intersection of plank and hull can theoretically be improved by adding large fillets as is done on the wing-fuselage intersection of a fast airplane.

Bowstay, shrouds, and whisker stays all create drag. Keep the diameter as small as adequate strength permits and keep the termination fittings neat and small or completely inside plank and hull. The halyard should be inside the mast or tight against the leading edge. Pennants or flags on shrouds or sail add drag.

If there are small items on the rig that do not lend themselves to good streamlining, use a heavy, smooth-surfaced adhesive tape to clean them up. Such tiny improvements could be the margin of victory. When sailing, keep as low as possible consistent with visibility and your ability to control the boat.

THE EFFECT OF WEIGHT

Other things being equal, the lighter an iceboat is, the faster it goes. Therefore it is good design to make all parts of the craft as light as possible yet consistent with strength requirements. The idea of having extra weight on the ends of the runner plank to inhibit hiking has not proven to be of value. The same amount of weight added to the hull or plank to increase its strength has the same stabilizing force and benefits the craft in other ways. Weight directly on the runners makes them cut the ice more on small bumps and fly higher in the air on big ones. Removable weights for use only on very windy days on smooth ice might prove valuable.

In a heavy wind an extra passenger in an iceboat will make it easier to handle and less likely to hike. But even in this case the weight is a disadvantage in racing. For this reason, a fair doubles race (two in a boat) should always require a certain minimum weight for the two occupants combined (say 300 lbs.).

In a gusty wind that drops below sailing speed occasionally, or in areas where there are islands or other obstructions to the wind, extra weight may improve the ability of the boat to coast a longer distance on perfect ice before speed is lost. This could be an advantage. In any case, extra weight detracts from acceleration and hence is a disadvantage in getting a fast start in a race.

TRANSPORTING AN ICEBOAT

Because conditions for iceboating are not predictable or likely to be best at any one place for the whole season, transporting the rig to better places is commonplace. Of course, regattas mean a move for all but the host club members.

By nature an iceboat is take-apart-able. It breaks down into the hull, plank, mast, sail, runners, and 1,001 other small parts. These are generally moved on a trailer or on a car top. In either case a spe-

***Figure* 31. Iceboat on trailer.**

cial frame to fit all the major parts is very worthwhile (see figures 24). The places that touch the iceboat parts are often covered with pieces of carpeting to prevent scuffing enroute. If you car top your craft, tie it well fore and aft and don't forget the red flag on the overhanging mast that is required by law in most states. Some superhighways and toll roads do not permit trailers. Others put thumbs down on overhanging top loads. So plot your route ahead of time and check with local police to avoid trouble with the law and delays. All the small parts and tools should be kept in a box that can be handled readily or dragged by a rope on the ice to where your boat is to be assembled. Runners can also be handled easier if carried in a special box designed for dragging. And don't forget the horses (see figure 33) !

Figure 32. Cartop iceboat rack.

Figure 33. Foldable horse.

3

Dressing for Iceboating

There is no sport colder than sailing or riding in an open-cockpit iceboat. Skiers and ice fishermen think they know cold wind, but wait until they get in a 50-knot blast of wind on a subfreezing day.

Starting from the top, you must wear a crash helmet. While accidents are not common, the boom is always close to your skull. Shrouds, runner planks, masts, and hulls do break on the best of iceboats and upsets and collisions can happen. You'll want a full-coverage type helmet with room under it for a knitted wool, head, and face mask. To protect your eyes from the wind, the hinged plastic visor that attaches to some types of helmets can be good. One problem with the visors is that they tend to steam up from your breath and it is difficult to wipe your nose without a blast of air in your face. If you open the visor at any speed it is likely to blow off. If you can solve these problems the visor is fine.

Ventilated ski goggles of an amber color or polaroid are excellent for iceboating. If you wear glasses, see that the goggles fit over them. For the body covering, get a one-piece, insulated jump suit with a long zipper up the front and an attached hood. You don't use the hood while sailing but it's handy standing around the ice and working on the boat with the uncomfortable crash helmet off.

You can wear complete street clothes under these jump suits and

Figure 34. Well-dressed skipper.

use thermal underwear or extra sweaters as you feel the need. On your hands you need mittens that are insulated well and flexible enough to handle the sheet. Such mittens are made for skiers and snowmobilers and are fine for iceboating. Foam plastic-lined mittens with soft leather exterior permit better sheet handling and steering than do fleece or wool-like liners. Some ice sailors wear fingered gloves for extra dexterity, but they sacrifice warmth to do so.

A string that goes from one mitten cuff up one sleeve and down the other to the other mitten is often used by little children to keep them from losing their mittens. Iceboaters can lose mittens too. It happens if the sheet loops around a hand and you have to pay it out quickly. It may be worth the trouble to you to use the strings, especially for racing.

For footwear, heavy duty arctics over regular shoes with wool stockings will usually suffice. Rubber-bottomed, cloth-topped, zippered sport boots with wool felt liners are even warmer. It is very important that the boots are waterproof. Working around the shore and on warm days you're bound to step in water sometime. Wet feet, which later freeze, are not comfortable and may result in frostbitten toes.

You'll need a really substantial pair of ice creepers for pushing the boat to get it started as well as for general walking and carrying things on the ice. The steel-studded, crossed-steel-strap type with fabric toe and heel straps to go over your boots are good. They are widely used by fishermen and available at fishing tackle stores. Probably the best ice creepers are those used by fishermen and trappers; they have steel-studded metal soles that fit around the whole front of the boot and hold on with straps across the instep and behind the heel. Rubber overshoes or arctics with the metal cleats used by golfers put in the soles are excellent for iceboating.

One small problem: When you meet an iceboater on the ice, will you recognize him back in a warm room? Also—iceboaters' etiquette does not require removing mittens to shake hands.

4

How To Sail an Iceboat

STOPPING

Even before a beginner learns to sail, he should know how to stop. So long as the wind is blowing, the only noncatastrophic means of stopping is to let the sheet out and steer directly into the wind. Let the wind do the job. For the last several knots of speed, the hand brake can be pulled on. It will help bring you to a dead stop. Then, as soon as you get out of the boat, go to the steering runner and put down the parking brake. Loosen the sheet so the boom can swing, if the wind should change. If you expect to leave it for a long time, play it safe and take down the sail. A change in wind can blow over the boat and cause damage to the mast and the runner alignment.

While sailing, keep in mind that you may have to stop. Always leave yourself room to head into the wind to stop.

YOUR FIRST SAIL

It is a good idea to have had a ride as a passenger in an iceboat before you attempt to sail one yourself. Should you take a ride, watch everything and ask the skipper lots of questions about what he is doing from moment to moment. It's far from obvious to the neophyte what an expert is really doing. Although he seems to be doing very little with either the sheet or the steering, he is much busier than he seems.

If conditions are good, try handling the steering yourself and have the skipper instruct you while he handles the sheet. Then you handle the sheet while he steers—and comments. An awful lot can be learned this way. Next, he may let you do both while he comments and crosses his fingers—ready to grab the steering or sheet from you if danger threatens.

Now for your first solo trip choose a day with a light breeze (10 knots or less) and the largest ice area you can find. The iceboat is assembled and the sail is up and you're headed into the wind. Flip up the parking brake (all the way) and get back to the side of the cockpit to start to push. See that the sheet line is loose and the free end is in place where you won't sit on it when you climb aboard later. Now steer to port or starboard and push until you are about 60° to 80° off the wind (see figure 26). Straighten the steering runner, pull in the sheet so the wind tightens the sail a little bit. Next push to get started, jump on the runner plank and climb into the cockpit and get seated. Pull the sheet in to pick up speed while holding the 70° heading. Your first turn should be into the wind and to a 70° heading on the opposite tack without changing the sheet. This is called *coming about*. Repeat this several times and then head straight into the wind and come to a stop. You may want to try using the hand brake to assess its effect. Practicing the stop early in your sailing career is good insurance.

Get out and push to the 70° heading again and make another start. This time after you have sheeted in to gain speed, make a very long, gentle turn through 90° to downwind heading of about 135°. Again, do not change the sheet during the turn. You will feel the thrill of acceleration and speed and the lessening of the relative wind as your heading exceeds 90°.

After running at this angle for a while, smoothly turn downwind and jibe to a 135° heading on the opposite side, still without changing the sheet. After this try a broad turn through the downwind direction (180°) and back up to 70° heading upwind.

If you are having difficulty keeping up speed, start watching the telltale. After each major turn slowly let the sheet out and pull it in on a trial and error basis until you get the telltale to an angle of around 18° to the hull centerline. It is normal for the boom to be right in close to your head when you're sailing properly. The boom goes out to about 30° from the hull centerline only during the start-

DIRECTION DEFINITIONS

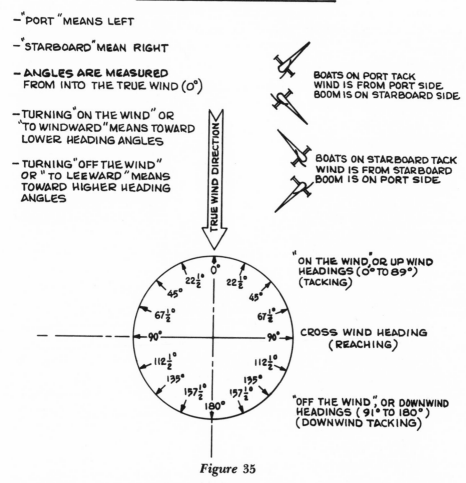

— "PORT" MEANS LEFT

— "STARBOARD" MEAN RIGHT

— ANGLES ARE MEASURED FROM INTO THE TRUE WIND (0°)

BOATS ON PORT TACK
WIND IS FROM PORT SIDE
BOOM IS ON STARBOARD SIDE

— TURNING "ON THE WIND" OR "TO WINDWARD" MEANS TOWARD LOWER HEADING ANGLES

— TURNING "OFF THE WIND" OR "TO LEEWARD" MEANS TOWARD HIGHER HEADING ANGLES

BOATS ON STARBOARD TACK
WIND IS FROM STARBOARD
BOOM IS ON PORT SIDE

TRUE WIND DIRECTION

"ON THE WIND," OR UP WIND HEADINGS (0° TO 89°)
(TACKING)

CROSS WIND HEADING (REACHING)

"OFF THE WIND", OR DOWNWIND HEADINGS (91° TO 180°)
(DOWNWIND TACKING)

Figure 35

ing up procedure which should be at a 60° to 90° heading off the wind. Once you're moving, it should be sheeted in gradually to about 15°.

Let it out if you slow down excessively and then work it in slowly. As you put in more hours and get the feel of your boat, you will want to try to get a maximum speed run on a heading of about 105° to 110°. Hold this heading and slowly sheet in to gain maximum speed. Give yourself plenty of room to run. The radius of the shortest turn you can make builds up as the square of the speed. If you are going very fast toward the shore, there is a point where it is impossible to make the turn. At 50 knots (58 mph) this point is about 220 feet from the shore for sharp runners on a perfectly balanced boat—even more for dull runners.

Before going out in higher, and gusty winds, please read the section of this book on gusts and on hiking.

To be a good sailor there is no substitute for practice. If you can ride with an expert and have him talk to you while you are skippering you may learn a lot faster. Hopefully, carefully reading this book and thinking about it even when you're off the ice will shorten your learning period.

THE TELLTALE

Attached to the bowstay of an iceboat about 18 inches from its foot is a 12- to 18-inch piece of ribbon called the telltale. A variation of the ribbon telltale is a feather mounted on the fore deck or the mast top like a weather vane (see figure 36). It's a good idea to use two ribbons in a race in case you lose one.

Brilliant orange or red is visible against the ice or the dark shoreline. The telltale is your only "flight instrument" and is extremely important if you are going to get the best out of your craft. The ribbon lines up with the relative wind and gives you a measure of the angle between the relative wind and the hull centerline. When sailing, the relative wind is always from the front quadrant (45°) of the iceboat. If you are coasting directly into the relative wind, the telltale aims straight back and you slow down. Starting up with the wind abeam, the telltale may be out at almost 90°. As you sheet in and gain speed, the telltale swings in to a small angle. Even when you are sailing downwind, because your speed is higher than wind speed, the telltale comes in to the same angle. The important thing to remember is that there is a nearly constant angle of the telltale which is most efficient for a particular iceboat. This angle is determined by the wind resistance of the iceboat and by the size and airfoil shape of the mast, sail, and boom.

The effect of extra drag on the runners makes this best angle slightly greater for light wind than for heavy wind. This would be most pronounced with soft or very rough ice, or misaligned or dull runners. Generally, though, the telltale angle at top speed should be the same for all normally used sailing headings relative to the true wind direction. The more efficient the iceboat, the smaller this "best angle" will be and the faster will be your speed for any wind heading condition. A typical value for the "best angle" is 18°. This angle can be found in your own boat by a trial-and-error process. Heading at 90° to a steady, true wind of 10 to 15 knots with the sail out, smoothly sheet in while watching the telltale. It will move in

Figure 36. Skipper's view forward.

as you gain speed up to your highest speed for the 90° heading. Where it stops moving in is your "best angle." Fix it in your mind by noting where it is relative to the edge of the hull or other mark. You might even paint or tape lines on the deck under the ribbon to denote its best position on each side of the center line. Now, whether you're tacking up or downwind or reaching crosswind, this is always the angle for highest speed. From then on the trick is to get the boat moving so the telltale gets into this angle.

If you notice the telltale moving out (a greater angle), it means you should adjust the sheet. Probably it means to sheet in more; but possibly, particularly on a downwind heading, you might have been too close hauled and should pay a little sheet.

If the telltale is too far in, it could mean you are heading too close into, or almost with, the true wind. The telltale too far in could also mean that you are coasting at higher than your best sustained speed. This could occur right after the wind slackened or if you headed directly downwind or upwind. In either case correct it by steering toward 90° to the wind.

In other words, the telltale is a tattle tale that tells right away when you are not doing right. You should let it be your guide after every turn to see that the sheet is where it should be. During any straight run, it will advise you of an adverse wind shift before you slow down. At the start it will show you whether you are headed in the proper angle to the true wind (60° to 70°) for fast acceleration.

A good sailor can keep the telltale in the best position at all times except during coming about and jibing.

When the wind is very strong (over 20 knots) or very weak (under 6 knots) you will have to compromise with the most efficient angle. In the strong wind, on headings of greater than 50° from the wind, the boat may want to go so fast at the most efficient telltale angle as to be uncontrollable. In this case you had better run with a looser sheet and luffing sail, taking in the sheet only enough to get the speed which you can control without regard to the telltale.

In a light wind, or in moderate wind on ice where the runners sink in so as to have a high resistance, you cannot get to the most efficient angle because extra sail thrust must overcome the runner resistance. In this case, for all headings you must let the sheet out a little further; and your best speed, tacking, reaching and broad reaching, will be slower and with the telltale further out. In effect, you will need to compromise best sail efficiency to get extra thrust to overcome runner drag to keep moving.

If this all sounds complicated, it is. You will find it very difficult to achieve this best angle of the telltale at all times. This is what is learned by lots of trial-and-error practice. It is also what wins races.

There are experienced ice sailors who do not use a telltale at all. By "the feel of the wind" and by sensing acceleration and pull on the sheet, they achieve the best sailing angle and speeds. Some of these persons learned by using the telltale. Others learned only by trial and error without it. However, if you are a beginner, don't ignore the telltale just because some champions can do without it. It's a great aid to learning and, to many experienced sailors, a key to perfection.

HANDLING THE SHEET

The sheet is the line that controls the boom angle. It starts at a fitting on the end of the boom and goes from there to the aft deck pulley, then to a boom pulley, then back and forth from deck to boom for as many pulleys are used. Next, it goes forward along the boom to a pulley on the forward end of the boom. Then it goes down through a ratchet pulley on the deck right below the forward boom pulley. The ratchet permits the pulley to turn freely as you sheet in, but does not turn when you pay out. The friction of the line in the ratchet pulley helps relieve the tension in your arms while holding the sheet against the wind pressure on the sail. The sheet line itself should be as large a diameter as will run in the pulleys. Three-eighth- and one-half-inch diameter lines are common. The line should be flexible so it runs easily through the pulleys, rough on the surface so you can hold it, and wear resistant so it does not chafe and weaken. There are many new types of synthetic fiber line being manufactured for sailboats that will do fine for iceboats. Before deciding on what you like best in sheet line, soak a piece with water and see what it is like frozen. Some ice sailors stick with old-fashioned manila or sisal because of its roughness. However, they lose their strength internally where they go over the pulleys before they look too bad on the outside and can break at embarrassing moments. More expensive sheet lines have parallel fibers inside wrapped in a woven cover. This gives extra flexibility with great strength and wear resistance.

For reasons explained previously, the sail of an iceboat is usually kept close hauled except for starting. It is let out or pulled in very much less often than in a soft water sailboat. For starting without pushing, head crosswind and let the sail out until it luffs. Then sheet in only enough to stop the flutter and the boat should start moving. Sheet in more as you gain speed until the telltale shows "best angle." So long as you don't select headings almost into the wind or downwind, you could ride around all day with the sheet cleated in this position. To do this, you should steer in very broad curves so that the telltale stays near its best angle. In effect, this is what a champion racer does when he runs his perfect race.

However, in a typical race situation there are obstacles—other boats to avoid, tacks to be made, and markers to be rounded—which dictate where you must head. These call for small sail adjustments. Most important are the adjustments in sheet required to get the best sail position by trial and error on any given tack. By keeping the sheet in hand at all times and sensing its pull, a good sailor can "play" the wind and get more speed than if he should cleat it fast.

If your boat steers with a tiller you can bend the sheet over the end of the tiller to remove the strain on your arms for short periods during the race but it is better to keep the "feel of the wind" in hand always. In pulling in the sheet very tight, it is sometimes easier if you grab the line over your head along the boom and "push" it forward with one hand, while your other hand pulls back on the free end.

If you are just sailing for pleasure and not racing, it is **OK** to use a quick-release cleat for the sheet. Be sure it is out of the cleat when you park.

The correct use of the sheet is most readily measured by the telltale angle in normal sailing winds as described in the section on the telltale. In very strong winds it is obvious that the sheet can be tightened only so much and still maintain control of the boat. When wind is over 25 knots you must often let the sail luff (lose shape and flap) or you will overturn the boat.

In a very light wind, oddly enough, you must also run with a looser sheet than in normal wind. If you attempt to sheet in to get a telltale to the most efficient angle you may have insufficient forward thrust to overcome the inertia quickly or to ever overcome the resistance of the runners on the ice. (This is more apparent if your runners are out of line or improperly sharpened so they drag.)

Beware of sheeting in too tightly (oversheeting) in a light wind on a reach (downwind tack). It happens most often in racing, when a sailor is eager to get everything possible from his boat, that he will oversheet and be gently passed by a boat with his sail further out. The telltale is useful in this situation since, when oversheeting on a broad reach, the telltale will move out at a large angle to the sail. This is your clue to let out the sail.

Pumping is the term given to pulling in sheet sharply and letting it out repeatedly. In a very light wind, when trying to accelerate from a very low speed, this will sometimes help. The sharp pull will accelerate the boat, while the slack sail period will still give thrust to maintain this speed for the next pull. This is more convenient though less effective, than getting out and pushing the boat to accelerate to a sailing speed.

HIKING

Probably no part of ice sailing gives a greater thrill to those in the iceboat and those watching than a long, high hike. However, an extreme hike represents an error by the sailor and loses time in a race. When a boat tilts a substantial amount, its sail spills wind and loses thrust. But if the hike is controlled so that the runner lifts only a foot or so off the ice, and slowly settles back, it can actually give an extra boost of speed (see figure 37).

Figure 37. (a) **DN in a controlled hike; (b) DN hiking higher.**

a

b

Hikes are generally initiated in one of three ways: by overpulling on the sheet while accelerating, by too quickly steering to a crosswind heading, or by a gust.

In a race, the thing to do when you find yourself in a hike is very easy to explain, but not so easy to do. Preferably you don't pay out sheet, but smoothly turn in the direction that will hasten you to the next marker. On a beat (tacking upwind) this means to turn into the wind. For tacking downwind (broad reaching) it means turning smoothly away from the wind. To do this requires that you have a good feel of your boat and plenty of courage. If the hike is an extreme one, you can always let go of the sheet and let the runner bang down on the ice. However, this causes a big loss of speed and can be very rough on the iceboat. A small amount of paid sheet has a tremendously big effect in a hike so try to let it out only a little bit at a time until you are back on three runners. Then, immediately start to pull it in again to keep your speed at maximum.

On a very windy day, a sailor who really knows his boat can tack with the windward runner just barely touching the ice with occasional lifting of the runner a few inches by playing the sheet and holding a steady heading. This can be the fastest way to get upwind when the wind is so strong that the boat's speed is limited by its stability. Continuous hikes of this sort are very tricky and should not be attempted in gusty air. See more under the section on gusts. Hiking is used by experienced sailors to pick up a runner to avoid a hazard on the ice. Work up your experience with hiking when you have lots of room on the ice. When the ice is soft or snow covered, the boat hikes much more readily because the boat does not accelerate as fast as on good ice. Danger of upsetting is therefore greater in case of a sudden gust.

In truth, an iceboat is very unlikely to tip over on a hike. When the angle gets extreme, the sailor is so aware of it, he usually lets go of the sheet in fear.

Beware that the sheet is not tangled in your arms, legs, or the boat, be certain you will not slide sideways in a hike and lose your ability to steer properly or fall out of the cockpit. This is not an uncommon occurrence for beginners.

GUSTS

Temporary wind speed changes are called gusts. They are very often accompanied by wind shift (direction changes). We'll consider only the speed change effect now.

If the wind slackens on either a windward or downwind tack, do nothing or steer a few degrees toward a 90° heading to prevent too much speed loss. If the telltale is in the right place there is nothing else you can do.

When the wind freshens strongly on any tack there is the tendency to hike. Here is where familiarity with your boat and courage can really help you. If the hike is not etxreme (plank to ice angle less than 15°), the best procedure is to ride it out with no change in sheet or direction. To get a feel of how steep a 15° hike is, with the iceboat parked, lift one end of the runner plank (onto a box or step ladder) by an amount equal to a quarter of the runner plank length. In the cockpit it feels much steeper than it looks from behind the boat. As the boat gains speed or the gust slackens, or both, the potential energy stored when the hull lifted is largely transferred back into kinetic energy (extra speed) as the runner settles back to the ice. Thus, the light gust gives you a nice extra spurt of speed. If the hike keeps increasing past 15°, smoothly turn toward the marker. This means into the wind on a windward course or with the wind on a downwind course. In all cases this improves your position on the course. When the gust abates, go back to your normal heading.

If you see a boat hike suddenly a short distance in front of you on your same heading, anticipate the gust by starting the turn before it hits you. You may be able to ride it out this way while he may have to pay sheet. If you can do this you will gain on him and maybe pass him.

When a gust raises the hike to 30° (it feels like 45°), there is no alternative but to pay sheet. Try not to panic and let go too much sheet causing the boat to fall back hard. This not only loses the shape of the sail and a lot of speed, but it is hard on you and the boat. As you gain familiarity and courage, you can let the sheet out smoothly and pull it back while holding a heading and keeping a low hike until the wind abates.

In summary, for a hike due to a gust:

1. For a low hike (15° or less), ride it out.
2. For a moderate hike, head toward the marker, for duration of gust then back to best course.
3. For an extreme hike pay sheet smoothly and get the sheet back in as soon as the wind abates.

5

Theory of Iceboat Speeds

When iceboating is being discussed, one topic almost certainly comes up: How fast do they go? In the late 1800s and early 1900s iceboating was among the fastest means of travel. It raced and could beat the railroad train, the automobile, and even the airplanes of that era. In these days of high engine power in land, sea, and air vehicles, and the tremendous speeds of space travel, the iceboat's claim to high speed cannot be taken seriously in an absolute sense. However, for the thrill of the feeling of speed, and the attainment of this feeling from a natural source (the wind), iceboating still reigns supreme. Because the iceboater is close to the ice surface and subject to high relative winds, the feeling of speed is enhanced and often misjudged.

Figure 38 shows the wind forces and directions on the sail. Heading in a crosswind direction, the speed of the boat combines with the true wind to give a much higher relative wind. This wind is deflected by the airfoil sail to give a substantial force at approximately right angles to the sail. Most of this force is trying to push the boat sideways, but the small forward component is enough to overcome the ice and wind resistance and drive the boat forward at a multiple of the wind speed.

With more perfect sail aerodynamics and reduction of runner and wind drag, the angle (23° in this example) can be reduced and the speed multiple increased for the crosswind heading shown. Figure 39 is a speed vector diagram that shows the effect of heading on

WIND FORCES & SPEEDS ON AN ICE BOAT

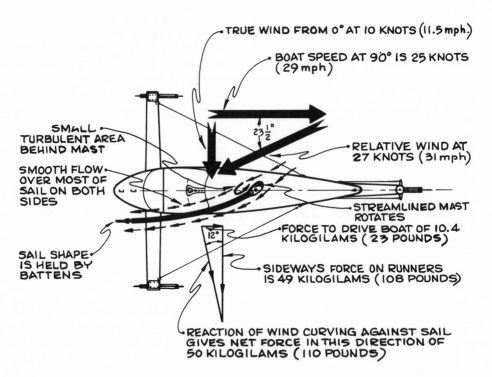

TRUE WIND FROM 0° AT 10 KNOTS (11.5 mph.)

BOAT SPEED AT 90° IS 25 KNOTS (29 mph)

SMALL TURBULENT AREA BEHIND MAST

SMOOTH FLOW OVER MOST OF SAIL ON BOTH SIDES

SAIL SHAPE IS HELD BY BATTENS

$23\frac{1}{2}°$

RELATIVE WIND AT 27 KNOTS (31 mph)

STREAMLINED MAST ROTATES

12°

FORCE TO DRIVE BOAT OF 10.4 KILOGILAMS (23 POUNDS)

SIDEWAYS FORCE ON RUNNERS IS 49 KILOGILAMS (108 POUNDS)

REACTION OF WIND CURVING AGAINST SAIL GIVES NET FORCE IN THIS DIRECTION OF 50 KILOGILAMS (110 POUNDS)

NOTES:
   THE FORCE TO DRIVE THE BOAT OF 10.4 KG. IS EXACTLY EQUAL TO THE AERODYNAMIC DRAG OF THE WHOLE ICE BOAT PLUS THE RUNNER FRICTION AT 27 KNOTS.

the speed for an efficient iceboat whose "best angle" is assumed to be 18°. This is typical of a modern Skeeter. In the diagram, the wind of 20 knots is from the north as shown by the thick arrow. The boat heading is a thin arrow and the relative wind a dashed line arrow. These situations are shown:

(a) The fastest speed obtainable occurs on a 108° heading. This is "south" of crosswind (90°) by the "best angle" of 18°. Note that in this case the relative wind is exactly crosswind (90°). Speed is 64.7 knots and relative wind is 60.7 knots.

(b) The best heading for getting downwind is on a heading of 144° from the wind. Here the boat speed is 52.3 knots of which 42.4 knots is in the downwind direction. Note that this is more than twice the wind speed.

BEST SPEEDS ON VARIOUS HEADINGS

NOTES:
  1 - THE ANGLE SHOWN AS 18° IS TYPICAL. THE MORE PERFECT
      THE ICE BOAT, THE SMALLER IS THIS ANGLE AND GREATER
      THE BOAT SPEEDS, 18° IS THE "BEST" TELLTALE ANGLE
      IN THIS EXAMPLE.
  2 - THE LENGTH OF THE SOLID ARROWS (VECTORS) ARE PROPORTIONAL
      TO SPEEDS OF THE BOAT OVER THE ICE.
  3 - LENGTHS OF DOTTED ARROWS ARE RELATIVE WIND SPEEDS.

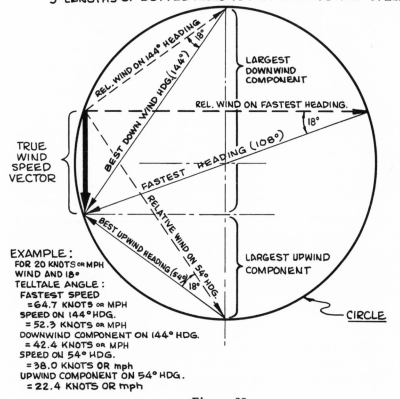

EXAMPLE:
FOR 20 KNOTS OR MPH
WIND AND 18°
TELLTALE ANGLE:
  FASTEST SPEED
    = 64.7 KNOTS OR MPH
  SPEED ON 144° HDG.
    = 52.3 KNOTS OR MPH
  DOWNWIND COMPONENT ON 144° HDG.
    = 42.4 KNOTS OR MPH
  SPEED ON 54° HDG.
    = 38.0 KNOTS OR mph
  UPWIND COMPONENT ON 54° HDG.
    = 22.4 KNOTS OR mph

Figure 39

(c) The best heading for getting upwind is on a heading of 54°
from the wind. Here the speed is 38 knots of which 22.4 knots
is the upwind component. This time note that this is a little more
than wind speed into the wind.

For those interested, the speed on any heading can be found on
the diagram by drawing the boat speed vector from the circle to the
point of the wind arrow. For the racer, it is important to note how
quickly the boat speed lessens on headings more into the wind (less
than 54°) even though upwind component lessens less rapidly. This

means that if you must "pinch," or tack close into the wind to reach the windward marker, you will lose a great deal of speed. On the downwind run, if you head at a lesser angle to the wind (more cross-wind), you will not be progressing downwind quite so fast but your speed across the ice and relative wind will increase. In a race this is safer than going too far downwind where you lose speed and relative wind to drive you.

When wind is higher than 20 knots in most areas, it tends to be gusty. When there are gusts the iceboat is subject to abrupt hiking, steering losses, and losses due to changes in the optimum shape of the sail. There is a definite top limit to the side forces on the sail, which can be handled before the boat hikes and spills the air, even in a perfectly steady wind. If it's made heavier to stop hiking, there is a point where the stays or the mast will break, the sail flutter or rip, or the battens snap. Further, as wind forces get higher, the sail does not maintain its best shape. Even when sheeted in hard, it gets less flat and a poorer airfoil shape.

Therefore we cannot multiply $3\frac{1}{2}$ times the wind speed as the wind speed increases to 40 knots and be assured of a 140-knot boat speed. So the speed claims and discussion go on and on with measured speeds of above 80 knots very rare. To measure speeds, set out a pair of markers carefully measured 2,000 feeet apart at an angle of approximately 108° to the true wind (see figure 40). This is the heading for highest speed. There must be at least another 1,000 feet on this heading for getting up to speed and 600 feet for turning after the speed course. Boats wishing to be timed should go upwind of the course and curve onto the speed run course. A person with a flag at the first marker lowers the flag as the boat passes the first marker. Another person, or preferably two persons, with stopwatches, times the interval in seconds between the flag drop and the time the boat passes the second marker.

Speed is computed by formula:

$$S = \frac{2000}{\text{seconds}} \quad \text{x .682 for miles per hour}$$

$$S = \frac{2000}{\text{seconds}} \quad \text{x .592 for knots}$$

Timing must be done very precisely because a one-second error is about 2.5 mph at 60-mph speeeds. On shorter courses, timing is even more critical.

It is difficult to get your absolutely highest speed in a specific

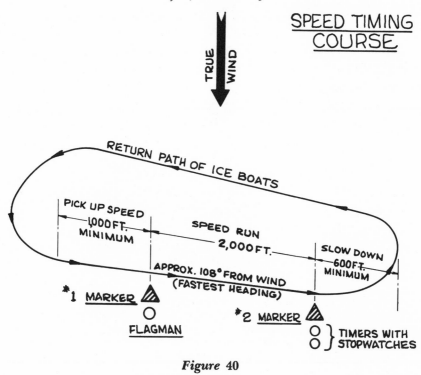

Figure 40

time and place. Hence the actual speeds determined on a speed check course such as this are often disappointing even when they are correctly measured.

To get a continuous speed reading, a low-range airspeed indicator from light airplanes that gives a measure of the relative wind can be installed. This, of course, is not the speed over the ice, but may be of interest and can be related to actual speed on any particular heading. The pitot and static pressure sources for these indicators are very difficult to locate and usually have significant errors. The pitot tube should be a sharp-edged piece of $1/4$" tubing with the open end aiming forward. Its pressure will be correct for relative wind angles up to about 15°. At higher angles airspeed will read too low. The tube must aim forward and be located in an area where relative wind is unobstructed. The static connection can be left open, if the indicator is placed in a cockpit out of the wind blast. If on the deck, use a piece of $1/4$" tubing closed at the end with a $1/16$" or smaller hole drilled in each side about 5 diameters from the front. This tube should also aim forward. A four-inch diameter wire brush on the shaft of a small DC generator attached to the steering runner has been used to measure speed. The brush is spring loaded to roll on the ice and spin the generator. This gives a voltage proportional to ice speed which can be read out on a voltmeter calibrated in knots or mph. On snow-free ice, this method gives a good speed accuracy, over a wide range of speeds, when properly calibrated. At 60 mph, the brush will turn about 5000 rpm and hence it must be reasonably well balanced or it will vibrate severely.

6
Safety

SAFETY ON THE ICE

Always check the ice before sailing. It changes from day to day and can be altered quickly by the sunshine, wind, and underwater currents. It's preferable not to check it alone; go out with a buddy and stay at least 50 feet apart as you walk or skate over the area to be sailed. Each of you should carry a long stick, a 20- to 50-foot piece of rope, and ice awls. Ice awls (figure 41) are made of headless nails stuck into 4-inch pieces of broomstick. By having the nails off center, a pair of these can be stuck together and carried in your pocket, to be used as described further on.

Ice creepers make walking easier and will help if you must pull your buddy out of the water (or vice versa, Lord forbid).

Black Ice

On that newly frozen, transparent ice sometimes called "black" or "green" ice, look for cracks to estimate the thickness. If it looks OK and does not crack as you walk on it, cut a small hole through to measure the thickness. Two and a half inches is marginal for iceboating and three inches is comfortable. Next, look around for any place that looks "different" and approach it with caution. Weak spots can be caused by springs, brooks, and pressure cracks. Check each area

***Figure* 41. Holding ice awls.**

and mark it with a bush or old tire so that you can see and avoid in the iceboat.

Gray or White Ice

Gray or white ice formed by melted-down, refrozen snow on top of old ice is weaker than the new, black ice mentioned previously. It can be fine to sail on because the runners get a good grip on it. Four and a half to six inches of white is considered good for sailing. Salt water freezes at about 27°F (−3°C) and can freeze into clear ice, which is weaker than freshwater ice. Usually however, ice on the salt water is formed by snow and ice crystals that are packed against a leeward shore by the wind and the accumulations of melted snow that form on this ice. It is very unreliable ice until it's almost a foot thick. Tides rise and fall and currents crack and undermine saltwater ice and make it very hazardous. While perfect clear, saltwater ice requires about 3 to 3½ inches for sailing, the usual, gray ice should not be used at less than 6 to 7 inches for ice boating.

The surface condition of ice is important to iceboaters as it often determines which runners to use. Clear, smooth ice demands sharp runners. Soft, snow ice suggests using wider and duller blades to keep from cutting through. Two inches of dry, fluffy snow on hard ice are fine for sailing, while a half inch of refrozen, wet snow will drag your speed way down and encourage the boat to hike.

Shell Ice

Shell ice is formed when water in a low area of ice freezes for $\frac{1}{4}''$ to $\frac{1}{2}''$ from the top and leaves a cavity of water or air beneath. A runner will cut through the top and make a frightful noise as it rips a slot in the thin layer. If the steering runner goes through, directional control is lost and the iceboat cannot be steered.

Where shell ice exists near open water, this can mean sailing helplessly into the open water. Where a rear runner is caught in shell ice, and a turn attempted, the runner or chock can easily be bent or the plank split where the chock bolts go through it. In a word: "Shell is hell."

Snow-covered ice, or even snow in patches has a special danger: it hides thin spots.

Good sound ice will crack and groan on a cold sunny morning. Don't worry so long as the ice remains flat. Pressure ridges (rifts) form either during a warm day or at night. In these the ice has been forced together so that a long overlapping crack is formed. This is usually, though not necessarily, across a narrow part of a lake or bay. Open water will appear in some areas along the rift, while at others there will be water a foot or so deep and good ice under it. Keep away from these pressure ridges! If you must cross do it near the shore and push the boat across. To be safe use the iceboat as a bridge and walk across the hull. Then pull the boat the rest of the way across with a rope.

Debris on the ice can be a real hazard. Cans and bottles, sticks, and stones will melt down into the ice and refreeze. Hitting one of these can dull a runner, knock it out of alignment, or cause you to lose control. Be alert for and assiduously avoid anything suspicious on the ice.

Spectators on the Ice

Spectators on the scene around iceboaters should be made aware of the hazards. Collecting in large groups will, of course, cause the ice to break. Trespassing on lawns and docks is not always appreciated by the owners. Spectators who wouldn't purposely trespass from a street onto private property will not even think about the fact that they are doing so from the ice. Also, it is considered very bad manners to touch anyone's iceboat without first asking. Skippers can be awfully temperamental about tamperers before a race.

Spectators, skaters, and snowmobilers are often unaware of the comparative lack of maneuverability of a speeding iceboat and of the width needed for the long runner plank. Both the skipper and the others on the ice should be alert and give each other plenty of room. Children, particularly, should be kept away from the race course. Photographers, who would attempt head-on shots or low-angle shots of a hiking iceboat should be made aware of the risk. Primarily though, the iceboat skipper must keep alert and keep a sharp lookout for people on the ice. Ice fishermen are a special hazard. The skipper must not only avoid them but also their tipups, garbage, and holes in the ice. But be fair and courteous; fishermen are also doing their thing and have a right on the ice too (even though most iceboaters will question this right).

Frostbite

Frostbite is caused by freezing of the toes, fingers, ears, or cheeks. It can happen at temperatures as high as 18°F (—8°C), when there is enough wind, and occurs in still air at lower temperatures. Frostbite causes pain in the toes or fingers when they are moved so it is quickly recognized there. On the cheeks and ears it may not be felt for a long time but it will appear as white or grey spots on the skin. Keep a watch out on yourself and others when in the cold, it can happen without your knowing it. The prevention is, of course, to wear warm enough boots, mittens, and face masks.

The treatment is to warm the affected part as soon as possible by placing it against a warm part of the body, getting inside, or soaking in lukewarm (105°F or 40°C) water. *Don't* rub or massage the area, apply hot water, or use the old, false "remedy" of rubbing with snow.

Drinking alcohol on the ice, or before going out, may make you feel warm, but it actually reduces your resistance to frostbite or freezing to death. Eat a nutritious meal and drink a warm beverage to keep warm for a day on the ice. Tea, coffee, or hot chocolate is fine.

SAFETY IN THE ICEBOAT

It is often asked about iceboating, "Isn't it awfully dangerous?" It is true, as with any sport involving speed, there is an element of danger that gives it zest. It is the conquest of danger by skill, knowledge, and care that lures a person to an action sport. The chief hazards to the skipper of an iceboat are: collision, breakup, upset, and going into the water.

Collision

Collision can occur between two moving iceboats or one and a fixed object. Collision between boats is very rare between skippers who know and use the rules of racing covered elsewhere in this book and use common courtesy to others while sailing. Riding or passing too close runs the risk of a gust hiking you suddenly and swerving you into another boat. Don't count on the other fellow to avoid you when crossing paths on opposite tacks. You may be on a starboard tack and have right of way to cut across his bow. But if he doesn't see you, doesn't know the rule, or is slow to recognize that the rule of giving way applies to him, you could be hit. Keep swiveling your head while sailing and always look back before coming about or jibing. Goggles restrict peripheral vision and heavy clothes restrict your neck bending so don't be a lazy looker. Keep alert for being in a three-boat trap in a race, especially near the marker. When a boat is coming on you from each side, the only way out may be to loosen sheet and pull on the brake.

Sail defensively—as if every other boat doesn't know the rules or can't see you. Shouting for room or right of way is very ineffective. Boat noise, wind, and the helmet effectively deafen a skipper. When overtaking another boat, you are always in danger of his sudden tack or jibe. Give him enough room!

Breakup

Much more than a sailboat, an iceboat is subject to tremendous forces on its rigging, hull, plank and chocks. Centrifugal forces in turns are tremendous, shock loads on all parts of the iceboat when dropping off a hike are many times normal loads. If an iceboat were made strong enough to take any kind of beating, it would be too heavy to perform, so its construction is a compromise between weight and strength.

Since an iceboat is often disassembled for transporting, there are a great many pins, clevises, bolts, etc., that could be improperly assembled and fail under stress.

As a result, it is not unusual for something to break while at high speed. Masts and stays snap under high gust loads. This usually is not serious if the occupants have crash helmets. A chock breakage on the plank with loss of a runner is also common and can be controlled by steering and loosening sheet. When a front chock or the steering mechanism fails, you're in real trouble. Without control you can hit something or you may head crosswind so that you hike up and upset.

The loose runner may go sideways or break off and leave part of the chock. This can catch in a crack in the ice and catapult the boat over, breaking the mast and dropping the hull on the sailor. This is probably the worst type of breakup. It can be avoided by routine careful inspection of the whole steering system and taking no chances on questionable items. If you sense the failure in time, drop the sheet completely, shield your face in your arms, and hope for the best.

When a runner plank breaks due to overload in the boat, a fatigued plank, or a sharp gust, it usually folds near the hull junction. If it breaks on the windward side, the shroud pulls the plank and runner up and it can easily fall on the skipper. Here again the helmet can be a lifesaver. If you notice you are riding lower to the ice than usual, your plank could be ready to break. Stop sailing and look for fatigue cracks. When the leeward half of the plank breaks, the boat usually drops over on its side but is cushioned by the sail as the mast approaches the ice. You have time to cover your face with your forearms and prepare for the slide to a stop.

The forces trying to snap a hull in two right under the mast are tremendous, so it does happen now and then. When you feel something crack drop the sheet and stop gently. If the mast becomes unstepped, it could fall on your head, so keep the relative wind to the side by steering to a crosswind heading.

Upset

Upset occurs when you are not quick enough to steer, or pay sheet on a hike, or if the steering breaks. Fortunately, the sail spills wind as it goes over and the boat tends to settle gently on the mast tip, bow runner, and one plank runner. Don't panic and keep the steering runner reasonably straight as long as you can. In a DN, Arrow, or other open-cockpit boat you will fall out, probably on the sail or boom. Your suit and helmet are your protection. In a tight Skeeter cockpit, you may be stuck in the boat until the end. So long as the mast and shrouds hold you are in no danger, but if the mast or shroud do break, you are in a very bad situation. For this eventuality, some Skeeter owners have built a raised backrest, or a roll bar which acts like a racing car roll bar to protect the skipper from being crushed (see figure 42).

In the Water

There comes a time in almost every iceboater's career when he goes in—partially or completely. You presumably are by now well informed on keeping away from suspicious areas and cracks, on not congregating in large groups on thin ice, on inspecting on foot

Figure 42. **Roll bar on two-place Skeeter.**

any new area or sailing around them slowly to look for bad spots, on not barreling into the setting sun on unfamiliar ice, on avoiding areas where brooks enter lakes, and on when to quit on a sunny afternoon when the temperature is 50°F and you're on saltwater ice.

Assume you have just experienced that sinking feeling and have three runners in the water. If you go in slowly in an Arrow or other floating hull, you're lucky. Keep your balance and get the sail down. The stays keep you from getting close enough to the edge of the ice to step out, so holler and wait for help. If you see you're really going in, fear and panic are your greatest dangers. There is practically no chance of your going under the ice. The boat will not sink entirely in most cases because there is enough wood to float the metal parts, so hang on to whatever is above water. Although cold water may take your breath away, you aren't going to be in serious trouble with the cold water for 15 minutes or more. The suit that kept you warm in the cold air has some buoyancy so you won't sink and it keeps you warm somewhat in the water. Even if it's bitter cold out, fresh water won't be below freezing and salt water only a few degrees below—so take it easy.

Swim slowly toward the edge of the ice (it must be near or you couldn't have gotten there) and put your arms on the good ice, give a couple of good scissors or frog kicks and you can slither up on the ice on your stomach. Don't try to lift your body on your hands. Stay low and snake your way onto the ice. Remember the water level is even with the ice; it's not like climbing onto a dock. A pair of small ice awls worn around the neck or in an outside breast pocket make getting out very simple. One in each hand lets you claw yourself right out on your stomach.

If help is coming with a rope or long stick, wait for them quietly rather than trying to get out alone. When they throw you the rope or hand you the stick, hold on tightly and let them drag you out horizontally. Don't try to help by crawling, you can help by kicking in the water. For those who would help someone in the water, they should come one, or at most two at a time. To get near to the one in the water, crawl on hands and knees with the rope or long stick. A second rope back to a helper behind you on good ice is good insurance for you. He will also help to pull the victim out.

Of course, if a light boat is handy and can be gotten to the scene quickly enough, the rescue is simple. At any regatta or club where thin ice might possibly exist, an aluminum dingy or small rowboat with a couple of spike ended poles for poling it across the ice is perfect. Two 50- to 75-foot lengths of rope should be in the boat. One with a lifesaver or floating cushion tied on and another to be used for pulling the boat back on the ice after it has gone in the water. Oddly enough, catching cold after a dunking is very rare so long as you get inside and warmed up as soon as you are out of the water. Let someone else start the iceboat rescue for you. Get a hot shower and into dry clothes and you will be much more useful at the "raising" ceremony. You will then probably want to protect your iceboat from overzealous, inexperienced onlookers who may be trying to get your craft out.

To sum up the items that make for safe iceboating—obey your sailing rules, keep the iceboat in good repair, don't push too hard on gusty days, and keep calm if you are dunked. Iceboating has a good history of safety compared with speed boating or skiing. Maybe the dangers are readily recognized by beginners and their fears lead them to caution and safety procedures.

7
Racing

KNOW THE RULES

Iceboat racing, as in any other competitive sport, is subject to rules. These rules have been developed over a 40-year period and are known as the National Iceboat Authority (NIA) rules. There are numerous associations that sanction and run ice regattas, such as the DN Association, the International Arrow Association, the International Skeeter Association (ISA), and the Eastern Ice Yacht Association (EIYA). While each may have different rules for qualification and scoring, all conform to NIA rules for the actual sailing rules given in Appendix A.

If you want to race, you must know the rules for your own and others' safety, as well as to learn how to win. Study the words and the diagrams and imagine yourself actually sailing while you read until the rules of right-of-way are thoroughly in mind. Put red and green marks on the port and starboard sides of your boom so you can recognize which tack you are on immediately. Don't let the rules scare you by their wording and apparent complexity. They are really all common sense and courtesy, as you will find when you study them. The only arbitrary rule is the starboard tack right-of-way and that is solved by the red and green marks on the boom.

Examples of specific rules for classes are given in Appendix D for the Skeeter class and Appendix E for the Arrow class.

PREPARING FOR A RACE

Winning in iceboat racing, as in most other competitive sports, is the result of many interacting factors. Obviously, the condition of the yacht and the skill and experience of the sailor are important. Less obvious but very important are his health and mental attitude.

Oh yes—and good luck—that's what you didn't need when you won and what you didn't have when you lost. Surely, chance plays a part in racing. There's the draw for position, there's the small stone on the ice that dulled your runner on the first lap; there's the gust that you missed, but which the winner picked up and ran right by you to finish first. These might really have been your bad luck, but what about the old sheet line which broke during the race, the pivot bolt that fell out of the runner chock, the broken batten you didn't notice until you sheeted in after the start, the time the clevis pin came out of a pulley? Were they bad luck, or could you have avoided them? That's all we'll say about luck except to note that champions seem "luckier" than the rest of us. Those things happen much less often to them.

Mental attitude before a race is a powerful weapon. A good attitude is a confident and relaxed one. This comes from a careful preparation of your boat and gear well in advance of the race. If you can come to the regatta site the day before, unload the boat, partially assemble it, and get a good night's sleep near the site, you are way ahead. You avoid early rising, the long, tense drive, and the heavy work of unloading on the day of the race. You're also less likely to forget little items. Now you can have time in the morning to finish the details of assembly, align the runners, and give a complete inspection before taking a trial run.

A permanent checklist of all items needed for a regatta is a good worry saver. Keep it in your toolbox and go over it before you leave home and before you leave the site after the regatta. A sensible diet helps too. Eat a good dinner and forget the partying—don't start off hungry either. Eat a lumberjack's breakfast and leave the flask of "schnapps" behind. For winners, race day is all business. Select your clothes by the weather, too much so you sweat is almost as bad as too little so you are chilled.

It goes without saying that everything on the iceboat should be as perfect as you can make it—runners sharp, honed and not bent, shrouds without broken strands; no split battens; sheet broken in, but not frayed; chocks greased; halyard sound, correct tension in foot and luff; all clevis pins and safety pins in place; the telltale OK (plus a spare in the toolbox) ; and steering gear perfect.

The best reason for being out early is to look over the course. Although the markers may not be put out until just before the race, you can sail around the approximate course as judged by wind direction and look for obstructions, bad ice, and quality of ice. Also try to ascertain where there are "dead spots" in the wind and the location of "chutes," where wind funnels through a gap in the hills or group of buildings.

While you're doing this, check the feel of the boat for runner sharpness and alignment. You may have one set of runners for hard ice, another for soft. You may have a heavy wind and a light wind sail. This is the time to decide which should go on for the race. Once the markers are up and if there is time, try to sail the course just as if you were racing. Memorize checkpoints on the shore to assist in getting your best course to reach the markers. Particularly, find the points where you should make your final turn to the markers. It is often difficult to see the markers when people are standing near them in red suits during the race. As described later, your run toward the marker is the most important part of the lap.

Be on time for the skippers' meeting before the race and listen

Figure 43. **Regatta Day morning.**

carefully. The course is usually described and a chart of the area shown. The number of laps and the areas to avoid are also specified. Remember them! Keep notes if necessary. Writing tends to inculcate them on your mind. Get your starting position number and locate it on the ice.

When your class of boat is called, go directly to your starting block, put on the parking brake and make a last inspection of all bolts, safety pins, battens, cables, and pulleys. See that your sheet is not snarled and that there is a knot about fifteen inches from the end so if the sheet slips from your hand, it won't go through the pulley and you can grab the end. Check the tightness on your creepers, clean your goggles, and don't forget the chin strap on your helmet.

COURSE MARKERS

The markers at each end of the race course must be visible for as great a distance as possible, must be firmly fixed so they will not blow away, and be of such material that they will not wreck an iceboat if inadvertently hit by a runner or plank.

A 6- to 8-foot hemlock, pine, or other conifer tree with some red cloth strips to increase visibility has been the traditional marker. A hole is chopped in the ice to fit the stem and it is frozen in place. Discarded Christmas trees provide a good supply of these in most areas. When trees are scarce and conservation considerations suggest not cutting trees, other markers are used.

The tripod shown in figure 44 folds for easy transporting and meets all of the requirements. For informal racing and practice, tall, rubber traffic cones spiked to the ice are OK. For a long course or a major regatta a police-car type flashing beacon atop an inverted tall, peach basket is the ultimate in markers. Alternatively, the battery can be placed on the ice ten feet from the marker inside the course, so as not to be a hazard if the marker is hit. Numbered starting blocks, usually made of sheet metal or plywood, are shown in figure 45. These are placed on the starting line to indicate each boat's rear runner position for the start of the race.

There are two course markers located a mile or more apart and directly in line with the wind. The race starts at the leeward end and normally consists of three laps run counterclockwise around the two markers. A third marker of different color from the main ones may be added at a position 120 yards to windward of the leeward marker and 10 yards to the left of the centerline. No boat is permitted to go between the markers on a starboard tack when approaching the leeward mark of the finish.

COURSE MARKERS

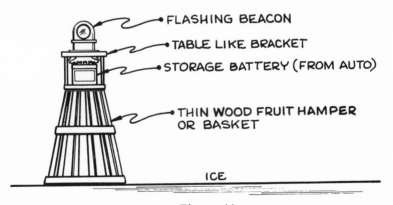

BOLT THROUGH LEGS

CONE OF RED OR ORANGE CLOTH SLIPS OVER TRIPOD

4'-8"

3 LEGS OF ½" LIGHT "CONDUIT" TUBING, 6 FEET LONG

ROPE

CHOP SMALL DEPRESSIONS FOR LEGS

HOLE IN ICE

CROSS PIN UNDER ICE

12"

FLASHING BEACON

TABLE LIKE BRACKET

STORAGE BATTERY (FROM AUTO)

THIN WOOD FRUIT HAMPER OR BASKET

ICE

Figure 44

STARTING BLOCK DESIGNS

BLOCKS NUMBERED ON 2 SIDES (I THRU 30)

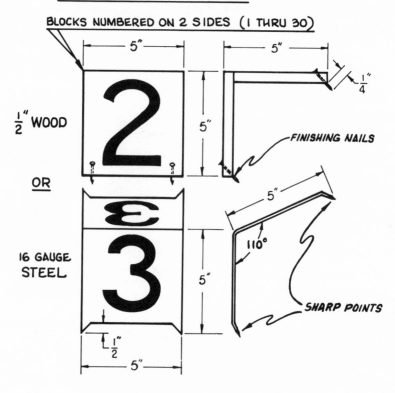

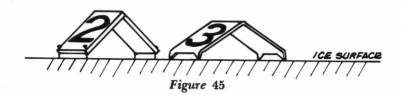

Figure 45

THE START

The boats are lined up as shown in figure 46 for the start. Positions are drawn by lot for the first race of a series. On subsequent races they are placed according to their finish position in the previous one. For a race with a large number of starters, positions 1, 3, 5, 7, etc., start to the starboard of the course centerline on a port tack. Positions 2, 4, 6, 8, etc., start to the port of the centerline on a starboard tack. For smaller groups or under special conditions, such as wind

Figure 46. Race start.

RACE COURSE

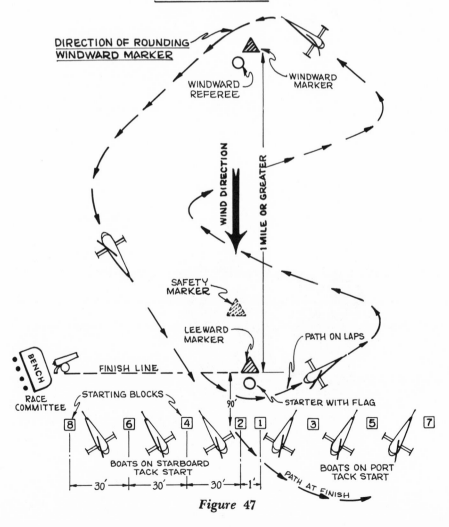

Figure 47

shift or ice hazards, the race committee may start all boats on the same tack. In most cases there is negligible theoretical advantage to being in one or another starting position. However, the number of tacks to reach the windward marker may be different and some of your shore checkpoints are different.

With your windward runner within a few inches aside of the marker and the sheet loose, head at 50° or more off the wind. If you are on the end boat and hence have room, it is better to head 55° to 60° off the wind.

With ice creepers on your shoes and parking brake off stand next to the cockpit on the windward side of the hull while waiting for the "go" signal from the starter. In a light wind take up the sheet tight so you are past the point where you get greatest forward thrust of the sail. To hold the boat back use the hand brake or stand with one foot ahead of the runner plank so it pushes against your leg. If there's too much wind so you can't hold your boat back or if it hikes while standing still, you must let out the sheet until you can hold it. Be sure the sheet end is neatly placed in the cockpit so it won't be snarled when you get in. Keeep your eye on the starter and raise one hand to signal him when you are ready to go. When the starter sees everyone ready, and he drops the flag or his arms—push! If there is a starting cannon being

Figure 48. Race committee.

used, don't count on it for your start. The dropped flag is the official start. The man on the cannon may be a second slow. That second can put you out in front. It is very important to gain as much speed as possible by pushing even in a good wind. Some sailors push until they can no longer keep pace with their iceboat and then jump on. (Sometimes they stumble trying to get on and lose the boat). As soon as you are in the cockpit, get the sheet in fast. Watch the telltale and get up to speed on a heading of about 65°. Then head up to your best tacking angle.

A special method of starting for the heavier iceboat classes in a light wind is sometimes used. The sheet is pulled in to sailing position and cleated in a quick-release cleat on the deck. Where no cleat is available, a slipknot is made in the sheet and the knot allowed to jamb in the ratchet pulley. The knot must be made so that a pull on the free end of the sheet releases it. The sailor then faces aft and holds the boat by the edge of the cockpit. At the start signal, he grasps the tail of the fuselage in both hands, lifts it and pulls the boat forward as hard as possible while turning toward it.

The lift gives him traction on the ice and permits a very strong pull. Then he must be quick to take a couple of running steps, then hop on the plank, yank the sheet to release the cleat or slipknot, and get seated. This maneuver takes a great deal of practice while away from other iceboats before using it in a race. There are definite risks of the boat getting away without its driver, of the boat taking a collision course with the next boat on either side, and of the boat hiking up by a gust while waiting for the starting gun.

The start is a likely time for tangling runners and collisions. Keep always aware of the boat on either side of you. If you have had to start at a 50° and want to fall off, either signal to your neighbor to the leeward or fall behind him. It will pay to do this, if he is tacking too close to the wind. Practice your start over and over again while not in a race, just to accustom yourself to the best way of jumping aboard and getting into sailing position.

On a windy day, you may find yourself on a slight hike during the initial accelerating phase. Don't panic or pay sheet or change heading. As you accelerate, the relative wind moves in and you may settle back off the hike ahead of your rivals.

Don't ride just behind and to leeward of another boat, you will be in his turbulence and lose speed. It's better to pinch up to windward of him if you can. If not, bear off to leeward and pick up speed. If you can pass him on the lee side, you can possibly head up again ahead of him.

Getting the jump on the start is a great advantage. It gives you the choice of headings and, if you are far enough ahead, the choice of when to make your first tack. So, you can see how important a fast start really is.

WORKING TO WINDWARD

Your best tacking speed is on a heading that is more than 45° off the wind (a typical value is 54°). It is a common mistake for beginners to try to hold heading at too small an angle to the wind thereby loosing some upwind speed component.

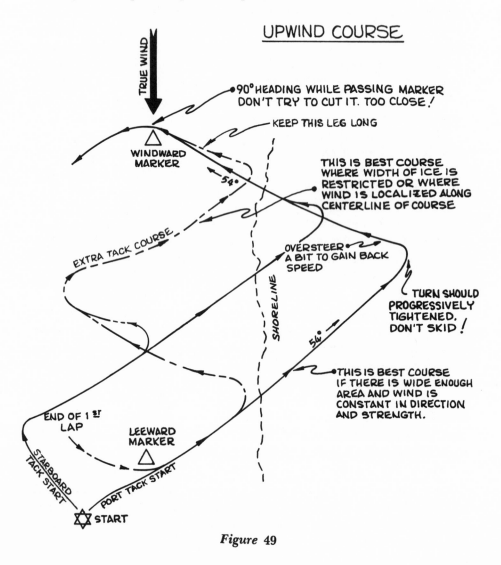

Figure **49**

When tacking, occasionally smoothly change heading a small amount into the wind. If you lose too much speed, slowly curve back off the wind until you feel you are on your best upwind heading. You will lose very little by this, but you will be testing for any change in wind direction and verifying your judgment of the optimum tacking angle. A similar trial-and-error procedure should be attempted with the sheet. Pull it in very tightly and hold a few seconds to note speed change. Then let it out a bit and see if it's better or worse. Watch the telltale! This is your indicator of performance and it should be at its proper angle as explained in the section on the telltale.

When you come about, pull the sheet in tightly as you turn and make the turn progressively tighter as you come into the wind and slow down. Don't turn so fast that you skid, but turn just as fast as possible without skidding. Remember a skid always wastes valuable momentum. Right after the turn, pay a little sheet and head off the wind further than your best tack would suggest. This gives the boat a chance to regain the speed lost in turning. Once you have the speed, smoothly turn toward the wind and sheet in to obtain your best up-wind heading.

If, during a tack, the wind abates, you may find it best to head off the wind a small amount. Don't wait until you slow down—remember keeping up speed is more important than holding the direction. If you start on a port tack and there is all the ice and wind you need to starboard, then hold this tack until you can reach the marker after one turn. You always lose speed coming about and this way you do it only once for the whole windward run.

Where you cannot make the windward run in one tack from a port tack start, make your tacks as long as you can, but try to finish the last port tack well to starboard of the marker. This way you can come at the marker on a long starboard tack. If you start on a starboard tack, figure it similarly. As a minimum you must come about twice. Try for this. If you can't make it, remember: make a long starboard tack to the marker, if possible.

At any time you are far off center, an adverse wind shift (see section on wind shift) has a more serious effect than if you are near the center. When the wind is shifty, you may not dare get too far off center of the course and might better take extra tacks. On a long course you may need more tacks to reach the marker. Keep them approximately equal either side of center unless some unusual ice or wind situation dictates otherwise. Keep testing for best heading and sheet position, and watch the telltale. There's no time to relax when working upwind; a winner fights it all the way.

ROUNDING THE WINDWARD MARKER

Many races are determined by a sailor's skill in rounding the windward mark. There are a few general rules to follow here:

1. While tacking upwind judge your turns so that you have a long enough starboard tack leg approaching the marker. Sometimes on the first lap, due to the direction of starting and the length and width of the course, you may find that you are almost reaching the marker on a port tack. In this case you must make your turn to starboard tack very close to the marker, hence, your speed at the marker will be reduced. It will then take you a long time to get back to speed on the downwind run. Remember what you did wrong the first lap and correct it by taking longer, or shorter tacks on subsequent laps so you will arrive at the marker on a long starboard tack.

2. Select your final upwind leg so you will be heading about 20 feet windward of the mark. One way to judge this while still on the port tack is to sight the marker in relation to the port runner. Usually it should be behind the runner. Just how far behind you must judge by your experience with how high your boat can point and the fore-and-

Figure 50. DN at the windward marker.

ROUNDING THE WINDWARD MARKER

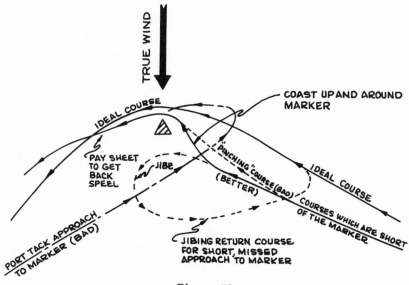

TRUE WIND

IDEAL COURSE

COAST UP AND AROUND MARKER

PAY SHEET TO GET BACK SPEED

JIBE

"PINCHING" COURSE (BAD)

(BETTER)

IDEAL COURSE

COURSES WHICH ARE SHORT OF THE MARKER

PORT TACK APPROACH TO MARKER (BAD)

JIBING RETURN COURSE FOR SHORT, MISSED APPROACH TO MARKER

Figure 51

aft relationship of your head to the runner. Find the correct angle by trial and error and stick to it. It is at almost the same angle even if the wind has shifted so that the wind is no longer in line with the markers. It is slightly further back on slow ice or very light wind. Be certain that you are on your "best" port tack before you turn to the marker. While there are advantages (see section on racing strategy) to having a long starboard tack to the marker, it is true that the longer this run is, the more serious is an error of judgment on when to turn toward the mark.

3. Smoothly turn off the wind as you approach the marker. When abreast of it you should be heading 90° to the course. If you turn so sharply that you skid, you are wasting momentum. Pass the marker with three or four feet to spare. Don't risk disqualification for hitting it. If you've planned your turn, there will be no need to shave it close.

4. After the turn don't head immediately to your best downwind angle, instead, slowly "peel off" letting the boat pick up to its maximum speed before heading to the best downwind heading. This means making a large smooth arc from well before to well after the marker. If your turn is perfect you need never change the sheet during this rounding. You may hike here, but don't panic. Just smoothly hasten your downwind turn.

We have talked about how to do it right, now we will discuss what to do if you have made an error, which everyone does at times. Let's assume you are on the approach leg and see you're too far leeward, to reach the marker. You can pinch the starboard tack tighter and move along at a much lower speed to just clear the marker. This leaves you with lost time and low speed at the marker. Better you head below the marker and tack at your best upwind course until almost to the marker. Then make a quick, nonskidded turn upwind and coast up to and around it with sail luffing. You still have low speed, but you have wasted less time getting there (if you make it). Look behind you before you make the upwind turn. Someone else may be bearing down on the marker at top speed. Since he is the overtaking boat, the rules say he must go wide of the mark and give you room. But don't count on it; he may not be expecting you to turn and just because he may be disqualified for hitting you, you don't win the race.

A third choice, if you are very short of the marker, is to continue the tack to a point directly downwind of the marker. Then come about, gain a little speed on the port tack, and make your next tack so it wraps you around the marker and starts you on your reach for the downwind leg. This is the least desirable course, it wastes a great deal of time and runs a risk of your fouling other boats at the marker. While you're on the port tack you must give way to those on starboard. Once you've come about for the run around the marker, you are the overtaken boat and boats coming in fast must go wide of you as described previously.

A fourth choice, when you're coming to the marker short, is to fall off the wind to pick up speed. Then jibe to port in a big, smooth U turn and head up until you are in position to make a second try at the marker. If this maneuver is correctly done, it can sometimes put you in a better position than the third choice above. This is because you have not lost speed, do not conflict with traffic, and have no sharp turns to make.

GETTING DOWNWIND FAST

This is the part of a race that separates the old masters from the neophytes. It is also the most enjoyable part of a race. To the uninitiated, going downwind would seem simple, but it is the trickiest part of ice sailing.

Coming off the upwind marker crosswind, you should slowly and smoothly turn to your fastest speed angle (see figure 52). When you

DOWNWIND COURSE

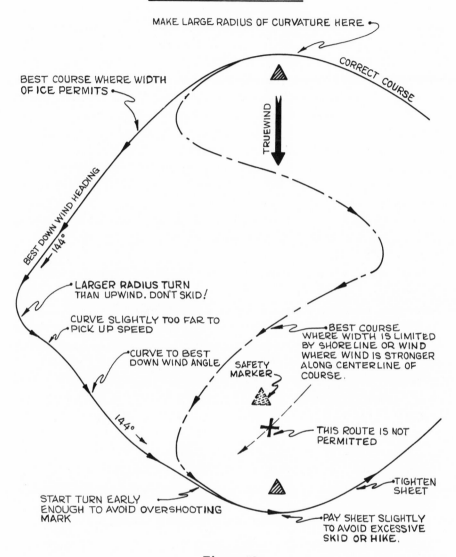

Figure 52

stop accelerating, bend your course downwind ever so smoothly and without paying sheet.

Your best heading is theoretically about 144° off the wind. However, if you turn too quickly to this heading you will lose speed that is very hard to regain. Instead, hold your heading first at around 108°, which is the direction for highest speed over the ice. When you feel you are no longer accelerating, smoothly turn off the wind keeping an eye on the telltale ribbon. It should stay right in the "best angle" position and the pull on the sheet should stay firm. If the telltale should move in or you notice the pull on the sheet slackening, smoothly turn back toward the 108° heading. It is very important that you do not let the speed slacken going downwind. It is better to go more crosswind and keep up speed than to head closer to the marker and lose speed. A good downwind heading for most conditions is about 135°. Only if you have a great deal of experience in your craft and ice conditions are good, with a true wind of about 12 to 15 knots, can you profit by the theoretically best course of about 144°. If you select a heading more crosswind than optimum, you will not lose much time on the downwind half of the lap. However, if you try to head too far downwind the loss of speed will be serious.

In changing from the starboard to port tack or vice versa (jibing), don't change the sheet. Just steer smoothly through the 180° heading to about 120°. After you have regained the speed lost in the turn, gradually increase your heading to 135° or higher, if you're that skillful. As in the upwind run, your best course is with just one turn halfway down the course, if the ice area is wide enough. There is one problem with the single jibe downwind run—you approach the marker on a port tack. This means you must steer clear of any boat crossing in front of you and steer wide of anyone jibing in front of you toward the marker.

Remember you must pass to windward of the safety marker on the starboard tack. If you pass short, (windward) of the course marker, you must head upwind, change tack, and go to windward of the safety mark before making another approach to the leeward course marker. This points up the importance of judging your approach to the leeward mark correctly.

ROUNDING THE LEEWARD MARKER

Near the leeward marker are the race committee and usually most of the spectators. So keep a look out for people on the ice. Plan your downwind zig-zags to approach the marker on a short, but comfortable port tack leg. It is dangerous to jibe right near the marker. (The safety marker, if used, prevents this.) You should be heading 20 to 30 feet wide of the marker as you stabilize on the final leg. As you approach the marker, start a gradual smooth turn so you arrive at the marker at a 90° heading with a few feet to spare. Keep swiveling your head to port to spot others converging on the marker. You will be at your highest speed at the marker and some skidding is unavoidable.

ROUNDING THE LEEWARD MARKER

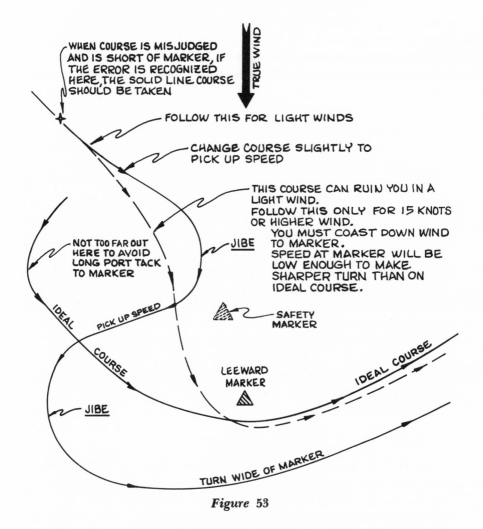

WHEN COURSE IS MISJUDGED AND IS SHORT OF MARKER, IF THE ERROR IS RECOGNIZED HERE, THE SOLID LINE COURSE SHOULD BE TAKEN

TRUE WIND

FOLLOW THIS FOR LIGHT WINDS

CHANGE COURSE SLIGHTLY TO PICK UP SPEED

THIS COURSE CAN RUIN YOU IN A LIGHT WIND.
FOLLOW THIS ONLY FOR 15 KNOTS OR HIGHER WIND.
YOU MUST COAST DOWN WIND TO MARKER.
SPEED AT MARKER WILL BE LOW ENOUGH TO MAKE SHARPER TURN THAN ON IDEAL COURSE.

NOT TOO FAR OUT HERE TO AVOID LONG PORT TACK TO MARKER

JIBE

IDEAL

PICK UP SPEED

COURSE

SAFETY MARKER

LEEWARD MARKER

IDEAL COURSE

JIBE

TURN WIDE OF MARKER

Figure 53

Your runners and hull are under great strain and you will probably have to pay a little sheet as you get to the marker. As soon as you've passed it, get to your optimum upwind heading and sheet in to hold your speed. Don't forget the telltale. It should be in the "good place" when you are back on course.

If you misjudge your final port tack so that you are aiming short of the leeward marker, you will be faced with the greatest temptation in the sport, that is, to bend downwind so as to make it. Resist the temptation except in very strong winds. With winds under 10 knots you will trap yourself into a situation where you may actually come to a standstill. It happens quite often, sometimes to the top sailors. What occurs is that when you turn too far downwind your thrust drops nearly to zero. You coast along with the relative wind dropping fast. Then you see you can't make the marker after all and you decide to jibe. This kills more speed; you head out on a starboard downwind tack but the wind "seems to" have died. You have slowed to near wind speed and don't know it yet. So you jibe back to the marker again on what looks like your best heading, but still no relative wind because you're too slow. Your only choice is to head back crosswind and possibly get out and push—and you feel so stupid with the rest of the fleet rattling by you.

What you should have done is this: when you first knew you were short on the final port tack leg, you should make a smooth jibe (watching for other boats) and get your drive back on a starboard tack. This may take you too far leeward, but it does get your speed back. Now, jibe again and sail for the marker, which by now may be crosswind or even slightly upwind. It's better than stopping.

On a good sailing day, you will tend to hike at the marker on a perfect turn (see figure 37). If so, pay out a small amount of sheet until you get on your best upwind tack and then sheet in again for the fight to windward.

WIND SHIFT: FRIEND OR FOE?

In all of the previous discussions on racing we assumed the wind direction to be consistent and in line with the course. Now let's consider the effect of changes in wind direction.

Assume the wind had been from due north with the course set up in a north-south line. Just before the start of a race the wind shifts 10° toward the northeast and stays shifted. The officials decide to leave the course alone and start everyone on a starboard tack. In this case the tacks will be of unequal length. You stay longer on the legs, which aim you closer to the markers. In this case, the starboard tacks upwind and the port tacks downwind are the long ones. Because of the unfamiliar heading angles of the hull relative to the course, there is a tendency to misjudge the place to make the final turns toward the markers. Just remember the angle between the runner plank and marker for normal wind and make your turn at exactly the same old angles both on upwind and downwind markers. Of course any landmarks you had picked out are all wrong after the wind shift. Be alert for the wind to shift back to its original heading when the markers were set up. It is when the wind shifts temporarily during a race that quick recognition of the shift and consequent action can enhance your position. Unless there is snow blowing, there is no easy way to see the true direction of the wind from a moving iceboat. There is no water surface to see and any flags or blowing smoke are too far away to help. But it is possible to feel it, if you know how. The real problem is to discriminate between a change in intensity (speed) of the wind and a change in direction.

Imagine you are on a port tack to windward and you feel the pull on the sheet slacken, the telltale move toward center, and possibly the sail luffs. This is a sure sign of a wind shift to an increased (clockwise) angle. You have two choices: turn to starboard to get back your thrust, or come about. If you had just turned onto the port tack and are still far to port of the centerline, fall off to starboard and hold the tack to somewhat past the centerline of the course or until you can reach the marker with the new wind direction. If you are near or to starboard of the centerline of the course on a port tack, come about quickly to the starboard tack. This takes advantage of the shift and results in a heading closer to the marker. Should the wind shift back to its normal direction, you will be upwind of a rival who didn't come about. If it doesn't shift back you don't lose anything. Naturally, the same situation exists on the starboard tack. Here a wind shift to a more counterclockwise angle (from north toward northwest) calls for coming about. An experienced sailor, when he feels the wind change, will come about with no hesitation and very little speed loss. Any delay in taking action results in rapid deceleration because of the high relative wind on your nose. Many a race has been won by a sailor "catching" this adverse wind shift and using it to his advantage.

More subtle is the wind shift in the favorable direction. Imagine again that you are on a port tack beat and you have the wonderful feeling of an unanticipated acceleration. Don't sit back and enjoy it. If it had been an increase in wind speed you would have felt the added wind in your face, the pull on the sheet, or you would have started to hike. When you get acceleration without the other effects, it was a wind shift in the counterclockwise direction (from north toward northwest). The right thing to do is to smoothly turn a bit into the wind to take advantage of the shift and ride that leg as long as you can. If the wind shifts back to normal, you want to have gotten as much as possible out of it. The need for action in a favorable shift such as this is less imminent than for the adverse shift. The seconds lost before you head further upwind will have given you extra speed, which is always for the good.

On the downwind run, say on a 135° heading on a port tack, a wind shift from north toward northeast is a favorable shift. You can feel the acceleration and you should smoothly turn starboard (toward the mark) to take advantage of it. On this tack a shift from north to northwest is the adverse one and can really ruin you, if you don't sense it. Because you are tacking downwind at a good speed and the relative wind and sheet pull are light anyway, the shift is not apparent. Your best clue is the telltale. If it deviates from its best angle toward the hull centerline, it means you are not getting proper thrust but are coasting downwind and gently losing speed. The cure is to turn to port until you feel the pull on the sheet and the telltale is back in position. It will probably pay off to head even further to port to pick up the lost speed before jibing to a starboard tack.

Not recognizing the adverse shift on a downwind leg in time under light wind can cause you to coast to a stop while the fleet breezes by you.

HINTS ON RACING

Where the race course is in a valley between two mountains and the wind is not directly in line with the valley, the strength of the wind tends to drop off near both shores but more so near the windward one. Plan your course to stay near the center, even if it means more tacks.

Where a gap exists in a mountain range, the wind blowing through this gap tends to form a jet of higher-than-normal surface wind. Look for these jets of high wind and take advantage of them in a race by taking short tacks and staying in the jet.

If you find your arms getting so tired you can't sheet in tightly enough, try grabbing the sheet above your head by the boom in one hand and the free end with the other. Now you can push the sheet forward with the upper hand and pull with the lower. This may enable you to get more force than pulling with two hands on the end of the sheet. It also uses different muscles so relieves fatigue.

If the wind dies during a race, you are permitted to push to get started as long as you push along the directions you would normally make your tacks. You cannot legally push closer than 45° to an imaginary line between the markers. Further, you cannot push past a marker. If the wind is dead, it is considered to be below sailing speed and hence pushing cannot be considered "to get started." However, when you feel the light breeze come up, push at 60° for upwind and about 120° for downwind starts—and push as fast as you can before jumping aboard. The one push may get you out of a dead zone.

It is advisable to have more than one set of runners at a regatta. Should you run over a stone and ruin a blade, you can switch to a good one between races. Don't forget to bring along a file and stone for quick repairs of small nicks between races.

On the light wind day don't stray too far from the centerline of the course. A light wind signals a probable wind shift; and you don't want to be caught way off to the side with an adverse shift.

Beware of oversheeting on your downwind legs. In the heat of a race this is a very strong temptation, especially in a light wind. Watch for a too far out telltale and pay sheet or head crosswind, or both, if you find you have oversheeted.

On a very windy day, you can risk heading downwind at a greater angle than is optimum for normal condition. If heading more downwind will save jibing once or more it may be worth the loss in speed, but only if the wind is strong.

RACING STRATEGY

As in most types of racing, the winner of an iceboat race is not necessarily the fastest boat. The tortoise beat the hare; the dark horse nosed out the favorite.

We have discussed the importance of details on the machine. Now what little things can the skipper do to improve his standing? Some things he can do come under the heading of "strategy." Use of strategy, of course, must be entirely within the racing rules, the spirit of good sportsmanship, and courtesy.

Make the Right-of-Way Rule Work for You

The right of way, when two boats' paths cross while both are working either upwind or downwind belongs to the boat on the starboard tack. Figure 54 shows typical paths of two boats that we will assume have exactly equal speeds. A's position in the draw, or due to higher placement in a previous heat, is closer to the center of the course. Assume they start together and come about at the same time and distance from the starting line. This will be at imaginary lines (1) and (2), which are parallel to the starting line. When they reach imaginary line (3), boat B can turn and round the windward mark. Boat A, of course, must continue a bit longer on his port tack to reach the same line that B is on in order to round the marker. If he does, he will arrive at point (4) at the same time as B. Since A is on a port tack and B is on starboard tack, A must give way and turn to starboard.

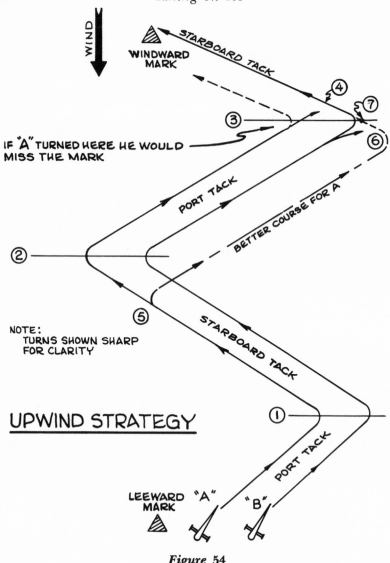

WIND

STARBOARD TACK

**WINDWARD
MARK**

④

⑦

③

IF "A" TURNED HERE HE WOULD
MISS THE MARK

PORT TACK

⑥

BETTER COURSE FOR A

②

⑤

STARBOARD TACK

NOTE:
TURNS SHOWN SHARP
FOR CLARITY

UPWIND STRATEGY

①

PORT TACK

LEEWARD   "A"
MARK   "B"

Figure 54

This wastes time and gives B a clear lead even though both boats performed identically up to this point.

To turn the tables, A had an option at point (5). Had he tacked sooner than B, he could have continued to (6) on port tack and there made his final turn toward the mark. In this case, at point (7) B would be on port tack and would have to give way to A. Then A would have a clear lead.

Going downwind, the situation is as shown in Figure 55. Assume

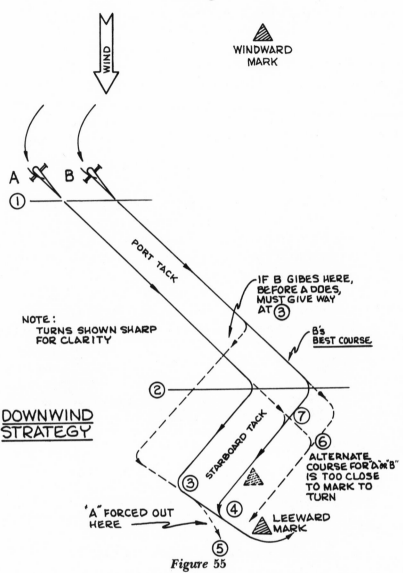

Figure 55

boats A and B are at line (1) and have exactly the same speed. They both jibe at (2). At (3), A turns toward mark. A moment later B reaches (4) and turns toward mark. B has the right of way because he is on the starboard tack while A is on port tack. As A gains speed after the jibe at (3) he becomes the overtaking boat at (4). Therefore A must give way to B on two counts: he is on a port tack and is the over-taking boat. B, by staying to port of A, has a clear advantage on the downwind leg. Had A continued straight at line (2) and jibed at (7) he would have forced B to overshoot the markers. B's other alternative would be to have jibed at (3) and to give way to A at (4), thus giving A the advantage.

For either boat to turn at (6) means going too close to the main marker for a good turn or going the wrong side of the safety marker, if one is used.

The general rule is to try always to stay starboard of your close competitior working to windward and to port of him coming downwind.

Following

It almost never pays to try to follow the person ahead of you for very long. If your boats are evenly matched, the leader has the advantage. If the follower makes correction in the sail or direction at the same time as the leader, he is doing it at the wrong time in relation to a gust or wind shift. If he waits to get to the point where the leader was when the leader made a correction, the wind condition might have changed here also. The correct strategy when you are behind a boat and can't seem to catch him is to do something different. After a marker, if he goes on a starboard tack, you go on a port. If there is an advantage to one or the other, you at least have a chance to beat him. By following, you're almost certain to hang behind, because to pass him on a straight run requires a significant speed advantage. Should he make an error in judgment on when to tack or jibe and you follow him, you both will tend to lose. A third party, thinking for himself, may then pass you both.

Covering

When you're out ahead and being hotly pursued by a single boat, you run the risk of your pursuer choosing a better course and passing you. If you could see exactly what he was doing and always take the same tacks at the same time he does, you would be likely to stay ahead. In soft-water sailing, this works very well. However, on ice, it is very difficult because of speeds and distances to watch behind you as well as to sail properly. In doubles racing, your crew can help on this, but alone all you can afford is a quick glance back from time to time. Nevertheless, if you do see your competitor on a different tack from yourself, it is wise to try to assure your lead by keeping always between him and the next marker. This is especially true on the last downwind leg of a race.

8

Skate Sailing

The skate sailor looks with amusement, and sometimes disdain, at the iceboater who spends so much of his time assembling and disassembling his equipment. The skate sailor can don his skates and rig his sail in several minutes and be off sailing while the iceboater works for half an hour or more with frozen fingers. Skate sailing had its beginnings in the early 1890s in northern Germany and Holland. It has progressed parallel to iceboating since then.

Conditions for skate sailing are the same as for iceboating with possibly thinner and somewhat smoother ice, but less wind, required. Equipment is lightweight, simple, and of course less costly than an iceboat. Speeds across the ice are surprisingly high, reaching over twice the wind speed with winds of 10 to 20 mph.

Except for the use of skates instead of boots with spikes, a skate sailor should be dressed the same as an iceboater. One other advantage the skate sailor has is that when the wind gets too light to sail, he can put the sail down and enjoy just skating.

The Sail

Figure 56 shows the typical construction and dimensions of a most effective type of skate sail known as the Hopatcong type.

When properly made and rigged, a skate sail should be stretched tightly on the spars and be perfectly flat and free from wrinkles. The

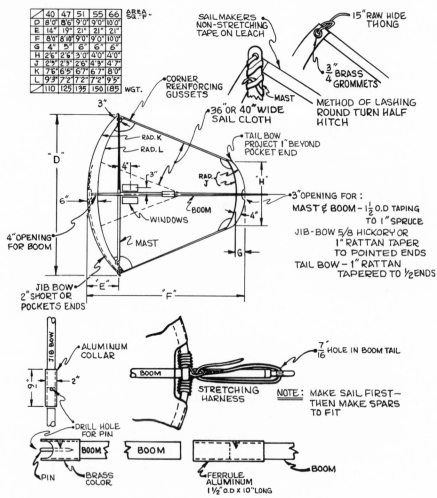

Figure 56. Skate sail design.

spars must be as strong as possible, consistent with light weight. They can be made in one piece for simplicity in manufacture, or can be made in two pieces joined by a metal sleeve for convenience in transporting and storing. Traditionally, Sitka spruce has been used for spars and rattan for the bows. However, aluminum alloy tubing and fiberglass are gaining in popularity. Likewise, the tightly woven cotton of yesteryear has given way to synthetics such as Dacron fabric and transparent Mylar sheeting for the sail itself.

The area of the sail should be in proportion to the height and weight of the sailor. The mast should be of a length that does not quite touch the ice while the boom rests on the shoulder with knees flexed in sailing position. A lightweight sailor must not carry so much sail area that he cannot control it in gusts.

The weights given in Figure 56 give good average weight for each size sail. A beginner would be advised to use the next smaller size.

The Sailor

To skate sail you do not need to be an excellent skater. You should be a confident skater, however, and have well-fitted skate shoes. Since you are usually sailing with both feet on the ice and have a sail to lean against, falls are infrequent. When they do occur, they are not serious except to your dignity. However, for racing and on gusty or high wind days, a crash helmet is good accident insurance. Skate sailing requires less physical effort than ordinary skating and it is enjoyed by those of all ages of both sexes.

The Skates

Racing, hockey, and figure skates all can be used for sailing. Racing skates are best for long distances and high speeds. Figure skates are easiest to control if you are accustomed to them but do not take rough ice or high speeds as well. Special, 18-inch tubular racing skates are used by the experts.

For comfort, the shoe must be of high quality to give proper ankle support. It should fit perfectly over only one pair of light cotton socks. Don't buy them so big that you can wear one or two pair of woolen socks in them to keep warm. If you do, you will have no ankle support and will probably cut off all blood circulation trying to get support by tightening the laces. Ordinary hockey skates are high off the ice and generally have poor ankle support. For these reasons, they should be avoided for sailing. Figure skates with the first tooth on the toe saw ground off can be fine. They should be ridden with the weight on the heels to be stable and to ride easily over bumps in the ice.

For cold weather, wear booties of felt-lined plastic, or leather, over your skate shoes and don't lace the boots too tightly.

Stop sailing now and then and do a little fast skating to warm up your feet and body.

Keep your skates sharp by wearing scabbords when leaving the ice.

Never walk on the ground or pavement in them. Skates must be sharpened with final grinding parallel to the blade, not across it.

They must not be put away wet or in wet scabbords. For storing, always dry carefully and coat the blades with oil or petroleum jelly to prevent rust. Sharp skates are essential for good sailing. Because distances are great compared with ordinary skating, they dull faster with use.

Handling the Sail

For your first try, select a day with a light breeze (5 to 10 mph) and at least a quarter mile square of good, smooth ice. Trying to learn on a windy day is very likely to end in a broken sail and a bruised sailor. Start with the sail lying flat on the ice with the spars upward and the front of the sail aiming into the wind. First pick up the sail in both hands by the jib bow, now turn it over and grasp the mast in both hands over your head and facing the wind. Your hands should be about three feet apart (see figure 57).

Turning to face crosswind, tilt the sail toward the wind to a vertical position so that the boom rests on your shoulder. Hold the mast with the windward hand only about 16 inches in front of your shoulder. The weight of the sail should balance on your shoulder (see figure 58).

Keep your skates about six inches apart with the one toward the wind ahead so that you are stable fore and aft as well as sideways. Keep your body upright and bend your knees. If you are standing correctly, your skates will be hidden from your view by your knees. As soon as the sail is brought upright you start to move. Pulling the mast closer to your chest will let the sail swivel into the wind and re-

Figure 57. Sails overhead.

Figure 58. (a) Skate sailor in good form; (b) skate sailor at top speed.

a

b

duce your speed. Pushing it forward will make the sail catch more wind and drive you forward faster. If the speed is too much to handle at first, pull the sail closer to you until the sail feels more controllable. If things seem to be getting out of control, reach up with your free hand and return the sail to the overhead position, as in starting out and turn directly into the wind. If things get completely unmanageable, drop the sail rather than struggle with it.

After a little practice you will find that you can relax a bit and enjoy the thrill of being pushed along crosswind by the sail with almost no effort. As a test, a well-balanced sail can be let go with both hands for a few seconds while you are gliding along in a crosswind direction. The wind holds the sail against your shoulder as you lean against it.

It helps to tuck the bottom of the sail in close to your skates while you are sailing. This not only makes it more controllable but also causes the wind to lift up on the sail thus relieving its weight from your shoulder.

To turn back to your starting point, first curve into the wind and bring the sail overhead to the starting position. As you continue turning past the direction straight into the wind, tilt the sail down vertically on the opposite (now windward) shoulder and head back crosswind.

After you have gained confidence on these crosswind runs, try tacking upwind. About 60° from the wind is about the best angle for getting to windward. Tacking closer to the wind is possible, but speed is sacrificed greatly and it is more difficult to hold the sail; getting downwind is easy. If you turn from crosswind to about 120° off the wind, your speed increases to double that of the wind in an exhilarating burst. The forces on the sail lighten and you whisk along with even less effort. On this heading with a steady 20-mph wind, a skate sailor who trims his sail perfectly may attain a speed as high as 50 mph. At this speed you must keep a sharp lookout for bad ice or objects that you might hit with your skates.

Always keep your weight on your heels while sailing. It tends to keep the skate from shimmying at high speeds and helps you to go over rather than through lumps and debris on the ice. Avoid snow patches; they may be deeper than they look, they may have sticky or refrozen snow in them, or cover thin ice. A snow patch can stop your feet while the rest of you keeps going.

When changing to the opposite downwind tack (jibing), don't lift the sail as when coming about upwind. The wind might get under the back of your sail as you slow down and twist it up over your head and out of your grip. Instead, keep the tail of the sail low and "roll" it over your back as you turn through the downwind heading to the opposite reach.

Figure 59. Jibing with skate sail.

Any time you want to stop, head into the wind and bring the sail to the horizontal position overhead in both hands.

As you gain skill, sail with your skates almost in line with each other, windward foot in front. Twist you body so as to flatten yourself against the sail to reduce wind resistance. You may even find it comfortable to reach back with your free arm and hold the back of the boom. This gives you better control while tacking in gusty weather, when the sail may momentarily be backwinded and try to blow off your shoulder.

Safety for Skate Sailors

From his higher vantage point, the skate sailor can more easily detect bad ice than an iceboater. Furthermore, if a skate sailor does go through thin ice, and holds onto the sail, the sail itself is good to hold onto in the water. It also gives a rescuer something to pull out with. Nevertheless, it is smart to carry a pair of ice awls just in case you get separated from the sail, as you go through the ice. If you're an inveterate thin-ice sailor (the first beautiful black ice is usually thin) you may want to wear a skin diver's wet suit jacket under your outer garment.

Visibility to windward is one of the skate sailor's constant hazards. Your sail should have a window of clear plastic and you should use it. There is a tendency to look only ahead and to leeward while sailing, Iceboats, snowmobiles, or skate sailors may be to windward of you and you could turn right in front of them when changing tacks.

Frostbitten toes can be avoided by booties over your skates and by taking time out from sailing and skating vigorously to warm up your feet and body once in a while.

Padding on the hips, knees and elbows sewed inside your clothes will make falling down less painful.

Even if you don't wear a rigid plastic crash helmet, a fur-lined cap offers a great deal of protection from bumps as well as the cold.

If you need glasses, try prescription-ground safety glasses. They'll take dropping on the ice and may save your eyes should you fall on your face.

All-in-all, skate sailing, despite its thrilling speeds, is a safe sport and can be enjoyed by enthusiasts from 7 to 70.

Skate Sailing Association of America

This organization since 1922 has been devoted to the interest of skate sailing. It provides information on where to purchase equipment, organizing races, and where the best ice is to be found. The secretary is Mr. Basil Kamener, 4 Manor rd., Livingston, New Jersey, 07039.

For more information see R. C. Jefferson's book, *SKATE SAILING,* published by Harrison Smith and Co., 520 Washington Ave. North, Minneapolis, Minnesota.

9
Organizing a Club

THE VALUE OF AN ICEBOAT CLUB

An iceboat club can offer a great deal to anyone interested in the sport. The camaraderie of individuals who enjoy the same interests may be the original reason for starting a club. If a clubhouse or meeting room can be obtained, it means a location for the bulletin board of activities, a place to discuss iceboating in bad weather and a place to get warmth and food. A club provides a base location for helping each other with mechanical problems, exchanging equipment and possibly a location of off-season social events. Having a telephone where any member can call to find out the ice condition is an invaluable service for club members.

Usually however, clubs are formed for club racing. This means having races every weekend and holiday and having a group to share the work of setting up and running the races. It is a fact that only by racing against others can you continue to increase your skill in sailing. The club provides the chance to race regularly at your most convenient site. It also provides a basis for running a regatta where outside sailors are invited.

Sometimes clubs are formed only for a specific class of iceboat. Others welcome all ice sailors and race all classes either simultaneously for separate scoring or in staggered heats.

Through club activity, new sailors can more easily be introduced to the sport. Some clubs have a regular hour each weekend where members with boats, which can carry passengers, are encouraged to give rides to spectators who just happen to be around. This often results in a convert to the sport and a new friend.

Clubs also make possible quantity purchases of equipment, which save dollars for members.

Appendix C is a sample of a typical constitution and bylaws suitable for an iceboat club. If you and a group of your fellow enthusiasts want to organize a club, use these as a start.

SPOUSES AND FRIENDS

An ice sailor can be male or female, married or single. Due to a human tendency to exist in pairs, which also affects iceboaters, there is often an accompanying individual at the sailing area or regatta. Ideally, this person should have the same unswerving devotion to the sport, the same willingness to endure cold and hunger, the same eagerness to carry heavy loads over areas of poor footing, even though the person does not get in the iceboat—except occasionally to humor the skipper.

Where friend or spouse is not inspired by the activities, don't despair. There are lots of other things to be done. The food and hot drinks must be dispensed. Scorers and other officials are needed on a race course. Somebody has to put out the markers and starting blocks. Or bring along a camera or a pair of binoculars. There are always things and people to watch and photograph on the ice. For the athletically inclined, there is often good skating in areas near, but not on, the iceboat course. It's a thoughtful move to pack some extra clothing and blankets for your buddy.

Appendix A

The Racing Rules of the National Iceboat Authority

PART I DEFINITIONS

When one of the terms defined in Part I is used in its defined sense in the definitions or rules, it is printed in CAPITAL LETTERS. All definitions rank as rules.

ACTUAL WIND—the natural wind.

WINDWARD-LEEWARD COURSE—a course sailed around two MARKS, an imaginary straight line drawn between the two MARKS is parallel to the ACTUAL WIND.

ON-THE-WIND—A yacht heading less than 90° from the direction from which the ACTUAL WIND is blowing is ON-THE-WIND.

OFF-THE-WIND—A yacht heading more than 90° from the direction from which the ACTUAL WIND is blowing is OFF-THE-WIND.

STARBOARD TACK—A yacht is on a STARBOARD TACK when the ACTUAL WIND is approaching from her right side.

PORT TACK—A yacht is on a PORT TACK when the ACTUAL WIND is approaching from her left side.

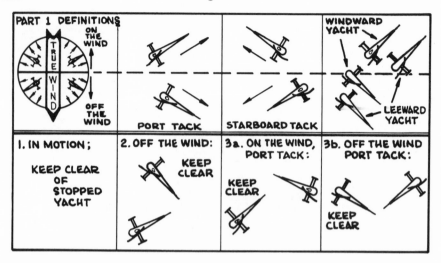

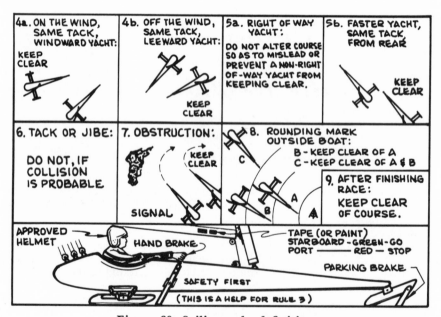

Figure 60. Sailing rule definitions.

WINDWARD YACHT and LEEWARD YACHT—When two yachts are on the same tack, the one on the side from which the ACTUAL WIND is blowing is the WIND-WARD YACHT, the other is the LEEWARD YACHT.

TACKING—A yacht is TACKING from the moment she is beyond head-to-ACTUAL WIND until her mainsail has filled on the other side.

JIBING—A yacht is JIBING when, with the ACTUAL WIND aft, the foot of her mainsail crosses her centerline until it has filled on the other side.

OBSTRUCTION—any object a yacht cannot safely sail over.

MARK—any object which a yacht must round or pass on a required side to properly round the course.

OUTSIDE—In rule 8 of the Right-of-Way Rules, any yacht to the right of another yacht is the OUTSIDE yacht.

CANCELLATION—A CANCELLED race is one which cannot thereafter be sailed.

POSTPONEMENT—A POSTPONED race is one which is not started at its scheduled time and which can be sailed at any time the Race Committee may direct.

ABANDONMENT—An ABANDONED race is one which is stopped while it is in progress and which can be re-sailed at the discretion of the Race Committee.

PART II MANAGEMENT OF RACES

A. Notice of races shall contain the following information:
   1. That the races will be sailed under the rules of the National Iceboat Authority and those of the association or class concerned.
   2. Date, place, or regatta and starting time of first race.
   3. Class or classes for which races will be held.
   4. Amount of entrance fee.
   5. Time and place of registration.
   6. Number of prizes.
   7. Time and place for receiving sailing instructions.
   8. Number of races scheduled and number required for a complete series.
B. Sailing Instructions
   1. May be written or verbal.
   2. Contents:
      a. Course location.
      b. MARK description.
      c. Starting time.
      d. Starting and finishing signals.
      e. Time limit of race (over-all time limit and time per mile for each class).
      f. Time limit within which and address at which protests shall be lodged and heard.
   3. Distribution—shall be available to each yacht.
   4. Changes—written or verbal changes to the sailing instructions can be made not later than two minutes prior to the starting gun.
C. Officials—duties and responsibilities
   1. Race Committee
      a. Personnel (course men, starters, timers, scorers)
         1. Course men:
            a. Determine if conditions (wind, ice, temperature, visibility) are safe; mark dangerous sections of ice.

  b. Supply MARKS and starting blocks.
  c. Set course (MARKS and starting blocks).
 2. Starters:
  a. Supply flags, loud speakers, audible signals.
  b. Start race.
 3. Timers: Time laps and the race.
 4. Scorers:
  a. Supply score sheets, pencils, master score board at head-
     quarters, tallies for drawing for starting positions.
  b. Are positioned in teams of two persons each, to windward
     of the windward MARK and at the end of the finish line
     opposite to the leeward MARK.
  c. Record the race as follows: Each team has a score sheet.
     The score sheet is divided into as many columns as there
     are number of laps in the race. As the yachts pass the
     MARK, one member of the team calls the sail numbers to
     the other member, who writes them down on the score
     sheet. A new lap column is started each time the leading
     boat completes a lap. After starting a new lap column,
     continue to mark all yachts in that column regardless of
     lap position until starting another lap column with the
     leading yacht. In the case of yachts which have been
     lapped by the leaders, the number of laps completed may
     be determined by the number of times such yacht's sail
     number has been tallied. After the last yacht finishes, the
     scorers must then work back through their tally sheet to
     determine which yachts, and in what order, finished the
     race properly.
  d. Post starting positions for succeeding race.
  e. Transfer race results to master score board and add up
     points.
  f. Determine final finishing positions in the series.
 b. Safety: The Race Committee should have on hand:
  1. First aid equipment.
  2. Phone number of first aid squad.
  3. Equipment for getting boats and persons out of the water.
 2. Judges
  a. Authority—have the ultimate authority over all other officials
     in all incidents involving interpretation and enforcement of the
     rules governing all aspects of the race.
  b. *Must* enforce all rules.
  c. Oversee the race and must protest all violations of the rules.
  d. Hear and decide protests.
D. Courses—all courses shall be WINDWARD-LEEWARD courses,
   MARKS left to PORT. See Appendix I for course diagram.
E. Starting
 1. It is recommended that the starting line be a line perpendicular
    to the ACTUAL WIND and set approximately 50 yards to lee-
    ward of the leeward MARK of the course and consist of marked
    positions. The center of the starting line shall lie on an extension
    of an imaginary line through the two MARKS of the course. Num-
    bered starting blocks (of two pieces of wood 5" x 5" x ½" nailed
    together to form a T; paint the numbers on the top of the T; lay
    the T blocks on their sides with the numbers facing away from

the course, i.e., to leeward; nails protruding from the edge will grip the ice) shall be placed along the starting line at intervals at least 2½ times the length of the runner plank, odd numbers running from the center rightward and even numbers running from the center leftward (standing facing the course).

b. The starting blocks do not rank as MARKS of the course.

b. The leeward MARK does not have a required side until a yacht has rounded the windward MARK for the first time.

2. Starting positions for the first race shall be drawn by lot (or shall be determined by another means if so announced in the sailing instructions) before the first race. Entries arriving after the drawing shall be assigned positions on the ends of the line. For succeeding races a yacht will start at the position corresponding to her finishing place in the immediate preceding race and DNF's, DISQ's, and DNS's shall be assigned positions at the ends of the line by the race committee.

3. Starting Procedure

a. At the starting line the Race Committee shall announce the course, number of laps, time limit for the race and for each lap.

b. Each yacht's windward runner is placed at the starting block, odd numbers on PORT TACK, even numbers on STARBOARD TACK if the PORT and STARBOARD TACK start system is used.

c. The Race Committee shall check to make sure all yachts are laid off (headed) similarly and the Committee has the authority to require a yacht to alter her heading.

d. There shall be a preparatory signal approximately 1 minute before the start. This shall be a visual signal made by the starter standing near the leeward MARK. He shall raise a flag or raise his arms. This may be accompanied by an audible signal (megaphone or gun).

e. The starting signal shall be the lowering of the starter's flag or arms. It may be accompanied by an audible signal. The visual signal governs the start, the audible signal is only a supplement.

f. After the starting signal, skippers may begin to move their yachts away from the starting line, either by pushing or sailing.
1. No yacht may be in forward motion at the starting signal.
2. A yacht that arrives at the starting line after the starting signal must come to a stop on the starting line before beginning the race.

g. It is recommended that when one class is lined up on the starting line when another class is racing, positions #2, #4, #6, #8, and #10 (the first five boats on the STARBOARD TACK) be vacated to leave room for yachts finishing to clear the finish line.

F. Finishing

1. The finish line is 200 to 300 ft. long and perpendicular to the ACTUAL WIND. It lies between a stake between the Race Committee and the leeward MARK. The Race Committee and stake are placed so that a yacht crossing the finish line from the direction of the windward MARK shall leave the leeward MARK on her PORT side.

a. The finish line shall be shifted at any time so as to remain perpendicular to the ACTUAL WIND.

2. A yacht finishes when any part of her hull or equipment crosses the finish line from the direction of the windward MARK.

3. The finish of the first yacht shall be indicated by the dropping of a flag by the Race Committee, this may be supplemented by an audible signal.

G. Time Limit

  1. Lap Time Limit—time allowed for sailing any lap of the course.

    a. The Race Committee establishes and announces the lap time limit. Individual clubs, classes, or associations may have a predetermined time per mile in their rules.

    b. If at any time during a race no yacht completes any lap within the lap time limit, the race must be CANCELLED or POSTPONED.

    c. Valid Race—A race is valid if any yacht makes each lap within the lap time limit.

    d. Example case: If the lap time limit is 9 minutes, the leading yacht must complete the first lap before the starting time (ST) plus 9 minutes. If the leader completes the first lap at ST plus 7 minutes, her time at the completion of the lap (L_1) is noted and the yacht leading (not necessarily the leader at L_1) at the completion of the second lap must complete that second lap before L_1 plus 9 minutes. (In this case, within 16 minutes of the starting time.) Her time is noted (L_2). L_2 plus 9 minutes is the time for *any* yacht to complete the third lap, and so on for each lap.

  2. Over All Time Limit—Any yacht not finishing within 30 minutes of the first yacht shall be designated Did Not Finish (DNF). This time limit may be altered by class, club, or association rules.

H. CANCELING, POSTPONING, ABANDONING, Changing Course

  1. The Race Committee may CANCEL, POSTPONE, or change the course before the start provided it informs all yachts verbally or in writing.

  2. The Race Committee may CANCEL or ABANDON a race after the start if a MARK has shifted or the course for any reason becomes unsafe.

  3. The Race Committee must CANCEL or ABANDON a race after the start if no yacht makes any lap time limit.

  4. The course may not be altered after the start.

  5. All yachts concerned shall be notified as to the date, time, and place of the resail of a POSTPONED or ABANDONED race.

  6. The signal for CANCELING or ABANDONING a race shall be the firing of a gun and the placement of a visual signal (flag, flare) at the leeward MARK.

I. Dead Heat—In the case of a dead heat in any one race, add the points for the place for which the yachts are tied and the place (or places, if more than two yachts are involved in the tie) immediately below the tied yachts and divide equally. Any yacht finishing immediately after the tied yachts shall be awarded the position corresponding to one worse than the number of yachts finishing ahead of her.

J. Accidents

  1. Each yacht must render every possible assistance to any yacht or person in peril, even if the person in peril is not racing. If in the opinion of the Judges any yacht not responsible for the accident

shall have thereby injured her chances of winning any prize, they shall discount the race or order it resailed.

2. A skipper of a yacht in distress shall make every attempt to signal all passing yachts and, if possible, the Judges whether he is seriously injured or not. If he is not, he should get out of his cockpit and stand up and walk around the yacht. If there is no visual signal of action on the part of the distressed skipper, the yachts passing and the Judges shall assume injury of a serious nature and CANCEL or ABANDON the race.

K. Re-sailed Races; When a race is to be re-sailed:
1. All yachts entered in the original race shall be eligible to sail the re-sailed race.
2. Subject to the entry requirements of the original race, and at the discretion of the Judges, new entries may be accepted.
3. Rule infringements in the original race shall be disregarded.
4. The Race Committee shall advise the yachts concerned of the date, time, and place of the re-sailed race.

L. Award of Prizes
1. Before awarding the prizes, the Race Committee shall be satisfied that all prize-winning yachts have complied with the racing rules, sailing instructions, and class rules.
2. If, within a 60 day period from the original date of award, the Judges shall find that a yacht did not comply with the racing rules, sailing instructions, or class rules, they may demand return of the award.

PART III GENERAL REQUIREMENTS

A yacht intending to race shall, to avoid subsequent disqualification, meet these general requirements:
1. Pay all required membership and entrance fees.
2. Meet the measurement requirements of the association sponsoring the race.
3. Shall not be sailed by a professional (s) ice yachtsman. A professional being defined as anyone who accepts money for sailing on an ice yacht. If the status of an ice yachtsman (as to amateur or professional) is questioned, the National Iceboat Authority shall be the ultimate authority in determining his status.

PART IV SAILING RULES

Any infraction of the following rules is cause for disqualification.
A. Fair Sailing—In all situations the Judges, Race Committee, and contestants must act in terms of common sense, safety, and good sportsmanship.
B. Right-of-Way Rules.
1. A yacht in motion shall keep clear of a yacht stopped.
2. A yacht sailing OFF-THE-WIND shall keep clear of a yacht sailing ON-THE-WIND.
3. When two yachts are sailing ON-THE-WIND, the yacht on the PORT TACK shall keep clear of the yacht on the STARBOARD TACK. When two yachts are sailing OFF-THE-WIND, the yacht on the PORT TACK shall keep clear of the yacht on the STAR-

BOARD TACK.

4. When two yachts sailing ON-THE-WIND are on the same tack, the WINDWARD YACHT shall keep clear. When two yachts sailing OFF-THE-WIND are on the same tack, the LEEWARD YACHT shall keep clear.

5. A right-of-way yacht shall not alter her course so as to mislead or prevent a non-right-of-way yacht from keeping clear. When a faster moving yacht approaches another yacht on the same tack from the rear, the faster yacht must not sail so close that the slower yacht cannot keep clear.

6. A yacht may not TACK or JIBE so as to involve the probability of collision with another yacht which, owing to her position or speed, cannot keep clear.

7. A yacht approaching and unable to clear an OBSTRUCTION without fouling or endangering another yacht may signal the other yacht for room to clear. The signaled yacht shall at once give room and if it is necessary for her to TACK or JIBE, the signaling yacht shall also TACK or JIBE immediately thereafter.

8. When approaching or rounding a MARK, an OUTSIDE yacht shall keep clear. Each yacht shall be entitled to room to cross the finish line.

9. After finishing a race, a yacht shall keep clear of the course and yachts still racing.

C. Sailing the Course
   1. A yacht shall be disqualified without protest if she starts prematurely.
   2. A yacht fouling a MARK (except when avoiding an accident), not leaving a MARK on the required side, or not rounding all MARKS in proper sequence, shall be disqualified.

D. Propulsion—A yacht may not employ any means of propulsion other than the action of the wind on the sails. However, the crew (unassisted by anyone except for reasons of physical disability as authorized by the Judges) may push the yacht to leave the starting line or to return the yacht to wind propulsion when necessary. Other pushing shall be cause for disqualification.

E. Ballast—A yacht must start and finish a race with the same ballast and crew.

PART V PROTESTS, DISQUALIFICATIONS, APPEALS

A. Protests
   1. Parties to protests.
      a. Who may protest:
         1. Any competing yacht.
         2. The Race Committee, or any member of the Committee.
         3. A Judge.
      b. Who may be protested:
         1. Any competing yacht.
         2. The Race Cimmittee.
   2. It is mandatory for all the parties in 1a. above to protest any infringement of the Racing Rules, Parts I, II, III, IV. A protest may not be withdrawn.
   3. A party entering a protest shall:
      a. Make his intent to protest known to the Race Committee imme-

diately after the race in which the rule infringement occurred or as soon as an infringement of other than the Sailing Rules is noted. A protest may be entered at a later time if the protesting party is unable to finish the race, but must be made within two hours of the finish of the day's racing unless the protesting party can prove, to the satisfaction of the Race Committee, that he was unable to meet the deadline.

    b. Present the protest in writing at the time and place indicated in the sailing instructions, stating the rule violated, a statement of the facts, and a diagram to illustrate same (when relevant).

  4. The Race Committee shall do its best to notify the protested party as soon as possible.

  5. The Judges must call a hearing as soon as possible, allowing a reasonable time for preparation of defense. Protests from one day's racing should be heard before the next day's racing begins and, on the last day of racing, before prizes are awarded. Failure on the part of any interested party to make an effort to attend the hearing may justify the Judges in dismissing the case or in deciding the protest as they see fit.

B. Decisions and Penalties

  1. The Judges shall make a prompt decision and notify, verbally or in writing, the parties involved.

  2. If, during the hearing, any yacht is found to have infringed any of the Racing Rules she shall be disqualified or otherwise penalized according to any special sailing instructions.

  3. If the Race Committee is found to have infringed a Racing Rule and a yacht's chances to win a prize were prejudiced as a result of the infringement, the Judges may order the race resailed.

C. Interested persons must not take part in decisions. No Judge may hear a protest involving a yacht he owned or sailed on at the time in question or involving a Race Committee of which he was a member.

D. Appeals to the National Iceboat Authority

  1. Appeals involving solely the interpretation of the Racing Rules may be taken to the National Iceboat Authority for final determination by any individual or group that is a member of the Authority.

  2. Preparation of Appeal Papers—All appeals shall be in writing and shall set forth the grounds of the appeal and be signed by the appellant. They shall be filed with the Secretary of the Authority within thirty days after the rendering of the decision appealed from together with:

    a. The written consent to the appeal signed by the Judges rendering the original decision.

    b. A copy of the sailing instructions.

    c. A copy of the protest.

    d. The names of the parties represented at the hearing, and of any party duly notified of the hearing, but not represented.

    e. A copy of the decision of the Judges containing a full statement of the facts found by them.

    f. An official diagram prepared by the Judges in accordance with the facts found by it and signed by it showing:

      1. The direction and velocity of the wind.

      2. Temperature and ice conditions.

      3. Visibility.

4. Positions and tracks of all yachts involved and their position in relation to the course and the MARKS of the course.

3. Decisions of Directors of the National Iceboat Authority shall be in writing and the grounds of each decision shall be specified therein. The decision shall be made within 30 days of the date the appeal was properly filed with the Secretary and shall be sent to all parties to the infringement and appeal. The annual report of the Directors shall contain all the decisions.

Sample Forms for Race Notices and Sailing Instructions (Part II, A & B)

A. Notice

(Name of Regatta)

1. All races will be sailed under the rules of the National Iceboat Authority and those of the *(class or sponsoring association)*.
2. The regatta will be held *(date)* at *(location)*. The first race will be held at *(time, date)*.
3. Races will be held for classes: *(class)*.
4. The entrance fee is *(amount)* per yacht.
5. Registration will be at *(headquarters)* on *(date)* from *(time)* to *(closing time)*.
6. Trophies will be awarded to *(how many places)*.
7. Skippers may obtain sailing instructions *(where, when)*.
8. *(Number of)* races are scheduled for each class. *(Number of)* are necessary for a complete regatta.

B. Sailing Instructions (distribute at registration desk or at skippers' meeting)

1. The course will be *(where the racing ice is in respect to place of registration)*.
2. The racing MARKS will be *(description of MARKS used for each class)*.
3. The starting time for each race:
4. The starting signal shall be the lowering of the starter's *(arms or description of flag)* approximately 1 minute after he raises his *(arms or description of flag)* to signify the preparatory signal. The finish of the first boat will be indicated by the dropping of *(description of flag)* by the race committee.
5. The time limit per mile for each class will be: . . . . Any yacht not finishing within 30 minutes of the first yacht shall be scored DNF.
6. Intention to protest must be reported to the race committee immediately after the race. Written protest must be filed with the Judges at *(where they should be filed)* within two hours of the finish of the last race of each day.

Appendix B

Constitution and Bylaws

SAMPLE CLUB CONSTITUTION AND BYLAWS

Article I

Section 1. This organization shall be known as .... Ice Boat and Yacht Club.

Article II

Section 1. The object of this organization shall be to promote, encourage, and stimulate yachting activities on ice and water in their respective seasons of the year and to further promote general public interest along the waterway known as ....

Article III

Section 1. The officers of this club shall be a Presidet, Vice President, Recording Secretary, Financial Secretary, Treasurer, Commodore, Vice Commodore, Regatta Committee, House and Grounds Committee, and Finance Committee.

Article IV

Section 1. The annual election of officers shall take place at the meeting of the club to be held the first Thursday of December in each year, this meeting to be known as the annual meeting. All officers shall be elected by ballot.

Section 2. Vacancies in any office may be filled by election at any special or regular meeting.

Article V
Section 1. There shall be a meeting of the club the first Thursday of each month, excepting June, July, and August.

Article VI
Section 1. The President shall preside at all meetings, call special meetings whenever he may deem it necessary and rigidly and impartially sanction and enforce the Constitution and Bylaws.

Article VII
Section 1. The officers of this club shall be a President, Vice President, in his duties and in the absence of the President to officiate in his seat.

Article VIII
Section 1. It shall be the duty of the Recording Secretary to keep a true record of the proceedings of all meetings of this club in a book provided for this purpose; to keep a correct roll of all members; to keep name and owner and register name with the club; to keep a correct list of each iceboat or yacht; to file documents, records, reports, and communications of the club.

Section 2. To notify each member upon his election and upon his becoming a member furnish him with a copy of the Constitution and Bylaws.

Section 3. To notify each member of each meeting. In the case of inability to attend any meeting he shall cause the necessary books and papers to be conveyed to the place of meeting and given to a competent person in the interests of the club.

Article IX
Section 1. It shall be the duty of the Financial Secretary to assist the Recording Secretary; to collect all dues, fees and other monies due the club, and pay same to the Treasurer, taking his receipt for same.

Section 2. He shall notify the Recording Secretary of all members in arrears on the first day of January of each year.

Article X
Section 1. It shall be the duty of the Treasurer to receive all monies from the Financial Secretary or any other person in the name of the club and to pay all bills contracted by the club from monies of the club.

Section 2. The Treasurer shall keep the accounts of the club correctly in a book provided for this purpose and his books shall be at all times open for the inspection of the members.

Section 3. He shall make a report at the annual meeting in December of all his receipts and disbursements of the amount of monies in his hands and of any financial obligation of the club.

Section 4. He shall deposit all balances in a depository designated by the club.

Article XI
Section 1. It shall be the duty of the Commodore to take command of the squadron and have charge of all club activities on water and ice.

Article XII
Section 1. It shall be the duty of the Vice Commodore to assist the Commodore in the discharge of his duties and in his absence to officiate in his place.

Article XIII
Section 1. It shall be the duty of the Regatta Committee to make arrangements for and act as judges in all regattas and match races.

Section 2. The Regatta Committee shall consist of the Commodore, Vice Commodore, five members and two alternates, who shall be elected at the annual meeting. They shall have the power to fill vacancies which may occur in their number and they shall have further power to appoint subcommittees to work in cooperation with them.

Article XIV

Section 1. The House and Grounds Committee shall be in charge of the clubhouse and all club property; they shall arrange for social affairs in the interest of the club and shall be general custodians of the club boats. Section 2. They shall report the conditions of the house, boats, or other club property whenever they find it to the best interest of the club to do so and they shall see that all necessary repairs be attended to at once and with the least possible expense to the club. The committee shall consist of five members.

Article XV

Section 1. The Finance Committee shall consist of three members and they shall audit the books of the Recording Secretary, Financial Secretary, and the Treasurer whenever they deem it necessary by the club and at least once a year make their report to the club at the annual meeting in December on the condition of the club's books at that time.

Article XVI

Section 1. All voting to be by ballot or viva voce at the option of the President or presiding officer, except as provided in Article IV and XVI.

Article XVII

Section 1. The names of all persons proposed for membership shall be handed to the Recording Secretary in writing at the first regular meeting of the club thereafter. Each application for membership must be signed by two members of the club in good standing. (Within this article provisions should be made for voting a member into the club plus initiation fee and dues payment.)

Article XVIII

Section 1. The membership of this club shall be divided into two classes —active and honorary. Active members are members who shall be subject to all obligations imposed by the Constitution and Bylaws. They shall (males and females) over 21 years of age or as specified by the rules of the club. Honorary members are members elected as a mark of courtesy and esteem. They have no voting powers at meetings and they cannot hold any elective office of the club.

Article XIX

Section 1. A quorum for the transaction of business at any regular meeting shall be . . . . members.

Article XX

Section 1. This Constitution may be amended at any regular meeting provided, however, that a notice of such amendment be mailed to each member (active) at least five days prior to such a meeting and then only by two-thirds vote of the members present at each meeting.

Bylaws

Chapter I

Each active member shall pay . . . . dues for the year to the Financial Secretary prior to . . . . of each current year. Any member in arrears of . . . . years of dues shall be suspended for . . . .

Chapter II

Notice shall be given or sent to each member of the regular meetings at least two days before the date of such meetings and of all special meetings if time will allow. Special meetings shall be strictly confined to the business or purpose for which they are called.

Chapter III

The distinguishing signal of the club shall be a pennant, a flag of distinctive formal and special significance. (Description of flag follows.)

Chapter IV

The Commodore's ice yacht or other yacht, when sailing shall wear the following colored pennant. (Description of pennant follows.)

Chapter V

In the event of the absence of the President or Vice President, the Commodore or the Vice-Commodore shall act in their stead. In the absence of all the above-named officers the members present shall choose a chairman for the meeting.

Chapter VI

Each member upon buying or selling an ice yacht or sailboat or upon changing the name of the same, shall give notice of the same to the Recording Secretary. No ice yacht or sailboat which is not registered on the club's record in the name of the owner or owners shall be entitled to representation in the club.

Chapter VII

There shall be an annual ice yacht race or other yacht race at the beginning of each season to be known as the "Commodore's Race," the time and place and distances shall be as the Regatta Committee shall direct.

Chapter VIII

In case of any gross violation of club privileges injurious to the welfare of the club shall at the next regular meeting of the club be given a fair hearing and at the discretion of two-thirds majority of the membership shall be determined the outcome.

Chapter IX

There shall be printed under the direction of the Recording Secretary all pertinent material of the club for the distribution of the membership at large.

Chapter X

At all regular meetings of the club the following order of business shall be observed:

1. Roll Call
2. Reading of the Minutes of Previous Meeting
3. Reports of the various Committees
4. Financial Secretary's Report
5. Recording Secretary's Report
6. Treasurer's Report
7. Reading of Bills and Communications
8. Resignations
9. Proposals for New Membership
10. Payment of Dues
11. Balloting for New Members
12. Old Business
13. New Business
14. Adjournment

Appendix C

International Skeeter Association

CONSTITUTION OF THE INTERNATIONAL SKEETER ASSOCIATION

Article I.

The name of the corporation shall be the INTERNATIONAL SKEETER ASSOCIATION

Article II.

The period of existence shall be perpetual.

Article III.

The object and purpose of the corporation shall be to encourage and promote amateur Skeeter Class ice yachting and ice yacht racing in all countries; to conduct races and regattas; to establish and enforce rules and regulations for the government of races and for the design and rigging of ice yachts in this class; and to accept donations of, to hold in trust or otherwise and to administer trophies and other types of property; and to carry on such other activities as may be necessary, proper or expedient in furtherance of the foregoing object and purposes.

Article IV.

No part of the net earnings or income of this corporation shall inure to the benefit of any member or individual.

Article V.

The number of directors may be fixed by by-law but shall not be less than three. The directors, other than the first board of directors, which shall be names in the Articles of Incorporation, shall be elected or appointed in the manner and for terms provided in the by-laws.

Article VI.

The policy of the International Skeeter Association shall be to cooperate with other ice yachting associations and to insure observance of the rules of the Skeeter Class; to strive to keep the Skeeter Class within financial reach of the person of moderate means, without restricting ability or encouraging neglect in conditioning ice yachts.

Article VII.

As an organization of individual members, the individual shall join through a Fleet on whose waters he normally sails. The authority to accept or reject applications for membership is vested in the Governing Committee.

A Fleet shall be an organized Ice Yacht Club approved as such by the Governing Committee. The individual Fleet's officers and government in local matters is not to conflict with the Association rules and policy.

If a Fleet has no I.S.A. members for a period of five years, the Fleet's call letter may be re-issued to another Fleet.

An individual not belonging to a Fleet may join the Association by proper application to the Governing Committee.

The powers of the Association shall be vested in the Governing Committee.

BYLAWS OF THE
INTERNATIONAL SKEETER ASSOCIATION

Article I. Dues

1.1 Each member shall pay annual dues of four dollars per year which shall be paid on or before November 15 of each sailing season.

1.2 The Association shall place in a special fund for the purchase of trophies for the annual championship regatta one quarter of the dues paid. Territorial divisions of the Association shall receive the direct proportion of this fund according to their proportion of membership in the Association except in years when the annual championship regatta is in that territory.

1.3 Members in active military service shall be exempt from dues but shall pay current dues and assessments if they enter the annual championship regatta.

1.4 The Eastern Division shall be alloted 50¢ per member to cover their operating expenses.

Article II. Fees

2.1 A registration fee at the annual championship regatta shall be paid by each entry in the amount of four dollars collected once each season by the host fleet and turned over to the Association Treasurer.

Article III. Voting

3.1 Each member shall be entitled to one vote at each annual, regular, or special meeting of the Association. Such vote may be cast by a delegate authorized to do so by a member Fleet.

3.2 Members in good standing, qualified to vote, are those on the membership list of the Association's Secretary-Treasurer as of ten days before the annual meeting.

3.3 At special meetings, or matters of the Association voted by correspondence, votes will be qualified on the memberships the individual Fleet had, or would have had, at the last annual meeting, with the exception of new Fleets, which will qualify the number of members at the date of the call of the special meeting.

3.4 Only authorized delegates and proxies shall vote, and must vote unless excused by the Chair. A majority of votes present shall decide all questions not otherwise stipulated. In case of a tie, the Chair shall cast one deciding vote. The Chair may also fix a time limit on speakers and motions to expedite the meeting.

Article IV. Delegates

4.1 The Commodore of each member Fleet, or his authorized representative, shall be responsible to present the Fleet's views and cast its votes at all meetings.

Article V. Meetings

5.1 The Annual meeting shall be held during the annual championship regatta, or at such time as the Governing Committee shall determine.

5.2 Special meetings, at the order of the Governing Committee, or upon demands, in writing, of twenty-five per cent of the membership, shall be held at a time and place determined by the Governing Committee.

5.3 The annual championship regatta shall have its dates and location selected by the International Race Committee. The preferred date, providing the Northwestern I.Y.A. annual regatta is postponed and conditions are suitable, is the third weekend in January, and not before, for three consecutive days, viz: Friday, Saturday, and Sunday. Every attempt shall be made to have a weekend intervene between the annual championship regatta and the annual Northwestern I.Y.A. regatta.

5.4 Three of the fleets in good standing shall constitute a quorum at all meetings. If a quorum exists at roll call, it exists throughout the session.

5.5 Notice must be sent to the last recorded delegate of each Fleet and to all members not less than five nor more than forty days prior to the meeting and if a special meeting, the purpose thereof must be stated in such form as to permit voting by mail and no other business may be transacted.

Article VI. Membership Eligibility

6.1 To hold office, to vote, to sail a Skeeter ice yacht, except as modified in rules governing the annual championship regatta, a member must be an owner, part-owner, or charterer of a Skeeter, and a paid up member in good standing of the Association, as well as a sportsman.

6.2 A member may be expelled from the Association for misconduct or flagrant infraction of the By-Laws, General Rules and Regulations of this organization by a ¾ majority vote of the delegates at a regular scheduled meeting and after he shall have been furnished an opportunity to be heard by the delegates in his own defense. No one who may have been expelled from the Association shall be re-elected or re-admitted to the Club for a period of one year, or until such time as appropriate restitution was made.

Article VII. Governing Committee

7.1 The Governing Committee shall consist of the following officers: The President (chairman), the Vice President, and the Secretary-Treasurer.

7.2 The Governing Committee shall call meetings, fill vacancies in office; act on memberships; approve all activities of the Treasury; and appoint all committees.

Article VIII. Officers

8.1 The officers of this Association shall be a President, Vice President, and Secretary-Treasurer. They are also the directors of the Association.

8.2 Territorial Divisions, such as the Eastern Division of the International Skeeter Association, will elect their own regional officers, their President to be officially a Vice President of the International Skeeter Association in charge of the Eastern Division. The duties of these division officers will be to administer the normal duties involving those of the division in the interest of the Association in that area.

8.3 All officers shall hold office for one year, or until their successors are elected, and shall assume duties for the ensuing year's business at the close of the annual meeting.

8.4 The President shall preside at all meetings of the Association and of the Governing Committee and shall have other duties as may be prescribed from time to time by the Governing Committee.

8.5 The Vice President shall preside, in the absence of the President, at all meetings, and shall perform any other duties as may be prescribed by the Governing Committee.

8.6 The Secretary-Treasurer shall record all proceedings of meetings of the Governing Committee and the annual meeting and any special meetings or meetings by correspondence. He shall collect the dues by sending out notices in proper time, keep records of membership, of member fleets, annual championship regatta standings, winners and awards, sail numbers; keep records of financial accounts, deposits, bank statements, disbursements as authorized by the Governing Committee; keep a custody record of all trophies and properties of the Association; and keep the legal affairs of the corporation to date and in order. The Secretary-Treasurer shall send out dues invoices in the first week of October each year and shall send out a second notice of dues in the first week of November each year with a request for an answer on whether or not the member wishes to continue or drop his membership. Each fleet shall be sent a list of that fleet's delinquent members at the time. Dues shall be payable November 1.

Article IX. Honorary Officers

9.1 A Commodore, who is the Commodore of the host fleet, shall be the liaison between the Association and the host fleet in arrangements for the annual championship regatta. He is to open and close the annual meeting and to be the Toastmaster at all functions.

9.2 Editor—to gather, write and publish the official news magazine of the International Skeeter Association, the "I.S.A. News & Views." The Editor is to be appointed by the Governing committee and shall continue in this duty until he or she requests termination. The Editor shall print the membership list and all retired numbers in the Fall Issue or the Winter Issue of the "News & Views."

Article X. Committees

10.1 A Nominating Committee, named by the President, shall submit a slate of candidates for each office, with this list to be published with the agenda for the annual meeting so that each member will receive a copy no later than December 15th of each year. This nominating committee shall be named no later than November 1 each year and shall promptly advise the Editor of the "News & Views" of their slate. Each nominee shall be seconded and voted upon separately by the fleet delegates. The candidate receiving the greatest number of votes shall be considered elected. Nominations may also be presented from the floor at the annual meeting.

10.2 The International Race Committee shall be appointed by the Governing Committee prior to the annual championship regatta.

(a) It shall consist of no less than five members and its chairman may or may not be a member of the host fleet, but its membership may include the Commodore.

(b) It shall conduct the annual championship regatta, shall have jurisdiction over all matters connected with the regatta, and supervise other officials and committees connected therewith, but its authority shall not extend to other matters or revoke the Governing Committee rulings.

(c) During the conduct of the annual championship regatta races the International Race Committee shall supercede the Governing Committee in the conduct of the racing, the layout of the courses, the appraisal of ice and racing conditions, and be responsible to the membership of the Association for the final scheduling or canceling of the annual championship regatta, advising the Secretary-Treasurer and the rest of the Governing Committee of their decision on this not later than 12:00 a.m. (noon) on the Wednesday (or the second day) prior to the first race day of the annual championship regatta.

(d) A trained or competent Official Measurer shall be a member of every International Race Committee.

10.3 The International Measurement Committee shall be appointed by the Governing Committee. It shall be in charge of all certified measures, grant or reject measurement certificates; issue duplicates; and answer questions on measurement rules.

10.4 The Trophy Committee shall be appointed by the Governing Committee. It shall be in charge of all permanent trophies and purchase all trophies for the annual championship regatta.

Article XI. Amendments

11.1 The Constitution, By-Laws, and General Rules and Regulations can never be suspended, but may be amended at any meeting by two thirds of the votes present. The basic principles of the Constitution cannot be changed, nor can an amendment be passed which will render ineligible a former yacht or active member whose eligibility was established under the then existing rules of this Association, and whose status cannot be changed to conform to the proposed amendments, nor shall retroactive legislation be passed affecting active members' or fleet's constitutional rights, except by a three fourths vote of the total voting strength of the fleets in good standing. If not present, a referendum can be ordered by the Governing Committee.

11.2 The Governing Committee shall have the authority to simplify, clarify, or correct the wording of any Article without changing its intent or purpose.

GENERAL RULES AND REGULATIONS OF THE INTERNATIONAL SKEETER ASSOCIATION

Part I. Rules Governing Sanctioned Events

Section 1. Racing Rules

1.1 All sanctioned races will be run in accordance with the Constitution and Racing Rules of the National Iceboat Authority and those of the International Skeeter Association for sanctioned events.

Section 2. Safety

2.1 The host fleet, in sponsoring a regatta or sanctioned event of the Association, shall not proceed unless there have been arrangements for adequate and speedy rescue and conveyance to hospitalization. In making known all regatta arrangements to the International Race Committee, this particular arrangement must be thoroughly detailed and approved.

Section 3. Course and Time Limit

3.1 The course, if possible, should measure not less than one mile between marks.

3.2 The race shall be a minimum of six miles, distance measured in a straight line between and around the marks.

3.3 The lap time limit shall be seven minutes per mile.

Section 4. Classification of Yachts

4.1 Yachts shall be divided into racing classes as follows:

Class A—Single place yachts, or two-place tandem.

Class B—Two place yachts, side-by-side.

Class C—Single place, two place tandem, or two place side-by-side yachts whose mast, when measuring along the mast, does not exceed 20 ft. 3 in. from deck to top of mast, including all mast and deck hardware.

Section 5. Names, Letters, and Numbers of Yachts

5.1 Each yacht shall carry on both sides of her sail a letter, 12″ high in a dark color, designating her fleet as registered with the Association and below this letter her number, also 12″ high in a dark color, as assigned to her by the Secretary-Treasurer of the Association.

5.2 The sail numbers shall be assigned by the Association and remain so until canceled by it or retired permanently by the Association. A member in good standing for ten consecutive years retains his number, and this number can be reassigned only upon release of the former owner.

5.3 Numbers are assigned to members, not to yachts. A member retains his number even though he may acquire a different yacht.

5.4 Each yacht shall carry on both sides of her hull a name, of the owner's selection, in letters not less than 3″ high, in a color contrasting to that of the hull side.

5.5 A one design class yacht may use its assigned class number on its sail in all I.S.A. sanctioned events provided it indicates such an intention to do so at the time of registration.

Section 6. Ownership of Yachts

6.1 No yacht shall be entered in any sanctioned event unless she is the bona fide property of a member or members of the Association. or

6.2 The person chartering a yacht shall be deemed the owner.

Section 7. Sails

7.1 Sails may be changed at will, except that at sanctioned events no more than two sails will be used during the entire regatta, unless specifically permitted by the International Race Committee by reason of irreparable damage to one of the original two entered.

7.2 All entries shall have their sails conform to one of the following measurement formulas:

The triangle shall be measured in one of the two following ways:

$$\text{AREA} = \frac{\text{AE X CB}}{2} \qquad \text{or} \qquad \text{AREA} = \frac{\text{AC X BD}}{2}$$

A	B	C	D	E
A	B	C	D	E

A — Top of pin in headboard hole. (Tape may be hung on this pin.)

B — After edge of sail at top of boom.

C — Junction of extension of after edge of mast and extension of top of boom.

D — After edge of mast.

E — Top of boom.

AE— Shortest distance, but E must not fall outside of B.

BD— Shortest distance.

7.3 The top of the eye in the headboard will be within 1 inch of the top of the headboard itself. The inner edge of the eye will not be farther out than 2½ inches from the after edge of the mast. No part of the actual headboard will extend over 5 inches from the after edge of the mast.

7.4 The roach will be measured by placing pencil marks 12 inches in from the after edge of the sail on every batten pocket, so that when a tape or a line suspended from the pin on the hoisting shackle and stretched taut to the after edge of the sail at the boom, it will be plainly visible if the roach is within or outside of the 12 inch limit.

7.5 Each Club or Fleet will appoint a sail measurer whose duties shall be to measure sails and certify with the Official Stamp all sails in compliance with the I.S.A. Rules.

7.6 The sail stamp is as follows:

ISA SAIL CERTIFICATE	AE	BC	Year
ISA SAIL CERTIFICATE	AC	BD	Year

7.7 A Skeeter is a cat rigged ice yacht having no more than 75 square feet of sail area in the triangle when measured in one of the two formulas described above, and with the following additional steps:

(a) Sails will be measured on the yacht and the spar as rigged for normal sailing conditions.

(b) A spring scale (ice or produce type) will be secured on the trimming (handgrip) end of the sheet rope, rigged through the blocks used in normal sailing conditions, and a steady tension of 70 pounds applied while sail is being measured and roach checked.

7.8 Re-cut sails must be measured and stamped.

7.9 Anyone doubting the legality of a sail may protest to the International Race Committee to have the sail in question checked, and if the sail in question is found illegal, the yacht shall be disqualified from the race in which she used the sail.

7.10 The yacht winning the annual championship regatta shall have her sails measured after the completion of the regatta and prior to the trophy presentation.

Section 8. Racing Restrictions

8.1 Each entry shall carry only a legal, stamped sail.

8.2 Each skipper must be a member in good standing of the Association.

8.3 Each skipper must wear an approved crash helmet during the entire race and each race of the entire sanctioned event.

8.4 Only one yacht registered under the same owner may enter a race or regatta. Scores made by different yachts of the same owner may not be combined in any series.

8.5 It shall be the responsibility of the race committee and, or, the International Race Committee and its appointed judges to check all entries at the starting line for complete eligibility regarding the skipper, crash helmet, stamped sail, etc. Ineligible entries will be refused a starting position.

Section 9. Crew

9.1 Not more than one person is to be permitted on a yacht during a race except by permission of the International Race Committee.

9.2 All persons starting a race must sail the entire race.

Section 10. Ballast and Equipment

10.1 All ballast and equipment carried at the start must be carried throughout the race.

10.2 No yacht may use shifting ballast.

10.3 No yacht may drag its main sheet on the ice.

Part II. Rules Governing the Annual Championship Regatta

Section 1. Procedure

1.1 The regatta shall be attempted to be sailed Friday, Saturday, and Sunday, beginning not earlier than 11:00 a.m. on Friday. The preferred date, providing the Northwestern I.Y.A. annual regatta is postponed and conditions are suitable, is the third weekend in January, for three consecutive days, viz. Friday, Saturday, and Sunday.

1.2 The decision to call or cancel a regatta must be made by 12:00 noon CST on Wednesday (or the second day prior to the regatta).

1.3 No races shall be started Sunday after 3:00 p.m. local time.

1.4 Registration closes at 10:00 a.m. Friday for drawing starting positions. Late entrants are to contact the International Race Committee for starting positions.

1.5 No more than 36 yachts shall start in any one heat. If after the racing has started late comers push the entries over 36, the regatta shall continue to be sailed under the single fleet system.

1.6 In the event of an incomplete regatta, it may be re-scheduled or transferred to another location. All completed races are canceled and the regatta starts from scratch on the later date.

1.7 After the regatta has been called on and entrants make the trip to the regatta and after two such weekends it has still not been completed, the regatta is canceled for the season.

1.8 Single fleet system if 36 or fewer yachts are registered:

    (a) There shall be attempted two races on Friday, two on Saturday, and one on Sunday, and in no event shall there be more than three races in one day.

    (b) Three races may constitute a regatta.

1.9 Split fleet system if more than 36 yachts are registered:
  (a) Three races (as opposed to heats) may constitute a regatta. If the regatta reaches the fourth and fifth race, any cancellation of consolation fleet races will in no way affect the validity of any championship fleet races.
  (b) Drawing for starting positions and heat assignments for the first race shall be in the starting area after registration has closed. Late entrants should report to the International Race Committee for starting position. Anyone who registers late and reaches the starting area after the racing has started may not sail in any heat in the race in progress unless the heat in progress fails to make the time limit or for some other reason is abandoned to be re-sailed at a later time. Likewise, a yacht that scores a DNF in a heat may not race in the opposite heat of that race.
  (c) The first race is sailed in two separate heats (A_1 and B_1). Each yacht's heat assignment is determined by the drawing.
  (d) The second race is sailed in two separate heats (A_2 and B_2). The odd position finishers in A_1 and B_1 (prior to protests) sail in heat A_2. They line up with the yachts from A_1 at the even numbered starting blocks. The even finishers in A_1 and B_1 (prior to protest) sail in heat B_2 and line up like in A_2. Any yachts scoring DNS or DNF in the first race are placed in alternate heats and alternate ends of the line by the race committee so as to keep the number of boats in each heat balanced.
  (e) The third race is sailed in the same manner as the second.
  (f) After the third race the points earned by each yacht in races 1, 2, and 3 (after protests) are totaled. The top half of the registered fleet (by points) will sail in the championship fleet for races 4 and 5. The remainder will race in a consolation fleet. In the event that yachts are involved in a tie that affects their placement in the championship fleet, all the yachts so tied may race in the championship fleet. For the fourth race yachts line up according to their point standings (1st, 2nd, etc.) and for the fifth race according to their order of finish in the fourth race.

Section 2. Scoring System
  2.1 Prizes shall be awarded on the basis of the total number of points earned for the regatta. The yacht having the lowest accumulated total number of points shall be proclaimed the winner, with each position thereafter determined accordingly. In the event of a split fleet system, both the winner of the A heat and the winner of the B heat will receive zero (0) points and so on up according to the table. All points are cumulative for all races. This applies not only to the championship fleet, but also to the consolation fleet. The winner of a consolation fleet race will receive zero (0) points and so on up according to the table, but in the final standings, the winner of the consolation fleet will be ranked immediately after the last place boat of the championship fleet even though his cumulative point total may be less.
  2.2 In the event of a tie, the tie shall be broken in favor of the yacht that has beaten the other the greater number of times. If a tie still exists, the tie shall be broken in favor of the yacht with the greater number of first places, then second places, etc. If a tie shall still

exist, similar championship prizes shall be awarded to the yachts remaining involved in the tie, and perpetual trophies shall be awarded on a divided time of retention basis and the trophies so engraved.

2.3 In case of a change in ownership of a yacht all points previously accumulated shall be canceled, and shall not remain with the yacht to the benefit of a new owner, nor remain with the owner to the benefit of a new yacht.

2.4 Each starter in each race (or heat) shall be credited with the number of points assigned her finishing place as indicated in the accompanying table. In all cases, no matter how many yachts are racing, the first place yacht receives zero (0) points and so on up according to the table. To determine the number of points awarded for DNF, DSQ, and DNS, a special definition of "last place" is used in the scoring system. The points assigned to "last place" will correspond to the number of registered yachts in the regatta. In a split fleet "last place" will correspond to one half the registered yachts. If an odd number of boats are registered, the next even number will be used, so that DNF, DNS, DSQ in all heats will receive the same number of points. If more than one half the registered fleet sails in the championship fleet, as the result of ties, see 1.9 (f), "last place" will have to be re-adjusted so that all DNF, DNS, DSQ scores for all heats and races will be equal. Yachts not finishing (DNF), not starting (DNC), or disqualified (DSQ) receive the number of points corresponding to one place worse than "last place."

2.5 If two yachts finish in a dead heat, both yachts shall receive the number of points for that place and the next yacht shall receive the number of points for the second position below that of the dead-heat yachts. If the dead-heat is for first and a trophy is involved, the trophy will be engraved accordingly.

2.6 A yacht that is involved in a collision with another yacht after the start and is thereby disabled and is clearly adjudged not to have been at fault and through the resultant disability cannot complete the prescribed course, shall receive the number of points applying to the finishing place one worse than the number of yachts which complete that heat satisfactorily.

2.7 Table of Points

Position	Points
1	0
2	3
3	5.7
4	8
5	10
6	11.7
7th place and thereafter	Place plus 6

Section 3. Awards

3.1 Keeper trophies will be awarded for the events as scheduled by the Governing Committee, to be paid for by the Association trophy fund.

3.2 Perpetual Trophies owned by the Association

(a) World's Championship Trophy—awarded to the winner of the annual International Skeeter Association championship.

(b) Skeeter Ice Boat Club 30th Anniversary Trophy—awarded to the runner-up in the annual International Skeeter Association championship regatta.

(c) Ladies' Championship Trophy—awarded to the winner of the ladies' series at the annual I.S.A. regatta. It is in an inactive status until such time that interest warrants scheduling of ladies' races.

(d) Lindstedt Memorial Trophy—awarded to the winner of the fourth race of the annual International Skeeter Association championship regatta. If only three races are sailed, it reverts to the third race. Under a split fleet system, it is awarded to the winner of the fourth race (first championship fleet race). If only three races are sailed, the winner of the third race heat who scores higher in the final standings is awarded the Lindstedt Trophy over the winner of the other third race heat. If there is no regatta completed but one or two races completed (in the final weekend the regatta is attempted), the Lindstedt Trophy will be awarded to the winner of the second race, or the first if only one race is completed.

(e) Siebke Memorial Trophy—awarded to the skipper who travels the farthest to race his yacht in the annual International Skeeter Association championship regatta. If, in the final weekend the regatta is attempted, there is no regatta completed, the Siebke Trophy shall be awarded.

Section 4. Finances

4.1 Prospective and actual host clubs for the annual championship regatta may submit to the Association Treasurer a listing of expenses incurred on behalf of the regatta. The Association shall reimburse each club up to a maximum of $50.00 per club.

Part III. Awards of Territorial Divisions

Section 1. Awards of the Eastern Division

1.1 Finch Championship Trophy—sailed for annually at the Eastern division regatta.

1.2 Fullerton Cup—sailed for annually at the Eastern division regatta.

1.3 Low Rig Trophy—sailed for annually at the Eastern division regatta.

Appendix D

The Arrow Ice Yacht

OFFICIAL TOLERANCES OF
THE ARROW ICE YACHT

The intent of the Arrow Ice Yacht is to be a one-design class in all aspects. The boat and equipment must remain as built by the Arrow Boat Company. No alterations to the rig or its equipment that would encourage unfair competition will be permitted.

FUSELAGE:
1. Fiberglass, supplied only by the Arrow Boat Company.
2. No alterations will be allowed that would change the positioning of the front runner, the location of the plank or the location of the mast. The center of the mast step shall be located 5'10¼" from the center of the rudder stock measured along the deck line. A tolerance of ¼" plus or minus is allowed.
3. Cockpit padding and back rests are optional.

RUNNER PLANK:
1. Length overall, including chocks (outside edges) shall not exceed 12 feet. Tolerance plus 0", minus 4".
2. Plank must be uniform in thickness throughout the entire length.
3. The trailing edge of the plank must be straight.
4. Plank must be wood, and Spruce is recommended; number of laminations is optional.

MAST AND BOOM:
1. Mast and boom of aluminum as supplied by Arrow Boat Company.

2. Tube length of the mast shall be 18'0", plus or minus ½".
3. The centerline of the bottom bolt in the hound fitting shall be located 12'1¾" from the bottom of the tube, a tolerance of plus or minus ½".
4. The boom tube shall be 8'9", plus or minus ½".
5. Floating boom connection is compulsory.
6. The standing rigging may not be altered to change the rake or list of the mast. The headstay shall measure 14'3⅝", the shrouds shall measure 14'7¼" pin to pin, plus or minus ½" tolerance.
7. No tube adjustors or links to lengthen the rigging will be allowed.

BLOCKS:
1. No more than six single blocks including a ratchet block may be used, while racing.
2. The diameter of the sheaves shall not exceed 3⅛".
3. The sheet line must terminate at the end of the boom.
4. Only one ratchet block can be used.

RUNNERS:
1. All front ends must be rounded to a ⅝" or larger radius.
2. Runners may be either ¼" or 5/16" steel and the total thickness shall be 1" between the chocks. Use of angle or stiffner below or outside of chocks is optional.
3. Length of the front runner shall not exceed 30".
4. Length of the side runners shall not exceed 34".
5. Height of the runners shall not be more than 5" nor less than 4½".

CHOCKS:
1. Standard chocks as designed must be used, and shall be fastened to the ends of the plank and must be located on the center line of the ends.
2. Opening of the chocks must be 1". Maximum thickness 5/16" stock.
3. No other means of fastening the runner will be permitted.

SAIL:
1. Sails purchased from the Arrow Boat Company are the only legal sails for the class.
2. Sails to be made of 6.5 ounce Bainbridge Dacron in 36" panel width.
3. Sail shall not be altered dimensionally.
4. A single 2' reef is optional. Plus or minus 2" is the tolerance.
5. Wood battens only permitted.
6. Only one sail shall be permitted in a regatta.
7. The legality of any sail that may be questioned dimensionally shall be checked in the following manner:
   The mid-point girth shall not exceed 5'9" measured flat and free of battens, sail must be dry when measuring.
   The luff and leach shall be measured on the boat with a tape hung on the halyard shackle and a 25 lb. pull on the sheet. The luff sail shall not exceed 15'9" to the tack pin, and the leach 17'0" at the clew.
   The foot length is controlled by the boom.

Springboards, foot steering, framing stays, removable ballast not permitted.

Bob Stay and strut are optional.

Hand brakes are optional.

Equipment changes during the regatta not permitted without the permission of the race committee.

Appendix E

International DN Ice Yacht Racing Association

OFFICIAL SPECIFICATIONS AND CONSTITUTION

A. FUSELAGE	PLANS	TOLERANCE	
		Plus	Minus
1. Length overall	144"	3"	3"
2. Beam	19½"	2"	2"
3. Thickness of decks and cockpit floor	¼"	0"	⅛"
4. Thickness of optional bottom	¼"	0"	⅛"
5. Sides and bulkheads	¾"	¼"	⅛"
6. Aft end of cockpit (intersection of seat back and floor) to pivot pin of steering runner	110¼"	0"	12"
7. Distance from bow to front of cockpit	60"	6"	6"
8. Stem block length	10"	Optional	
9. Stem width at bow	2¾"	1"	¾"

10. Stern block length   4¼″   Optional

11. Stern width at stern   1¼″   2¾″   0″

12. Seat backs shall be raked aft at an angle of 45 degrees plus or minus 10 degrees. They may be hinged for access to stowage compartment.

13. Seats shall be flat measuring 11″ in length at centerline; no maximum height.

14. Depth of side panel at each fuselage station shall not be less than heights in "Layout of Side Panel" on plans.

15. A. Bottom heights of side panels shall not exceed a maximum of 1″ above zero line and/or a maximum of ½″ below zero line. Zero line shall be established by a straight line tangent to stem and stern on bottom.

    B. Maximum height of side panels above zero line may be 8½″ including deck and bottom covering. All maximum heights of side panels shall be proportional to height as shown in "Layout of Side Panel" on plans.

16. Hull cross sections must be rectangular from a point 6″ from the bow to a point 6″ from stern.

17. Cockpit floor shall be installed as shown in plans; cockpit bottom *must* be on top of listings. A minimum of 2 knees must be installed.

18. Structural members such as longerons, stringers, knees, listings, bulkheads, bottom, deck, etc. may be added.

19. Design of the internal structure of the fuselage is optional.

20. Grab rails may be installed on the outside vertical surface of the side panels. They may not exceed beyond 8″ either end of cockpit. Rails shall not exceed 1″ in depth or width. Rails are exempted from fuselage measurements.

21. Steering post and chock may be inclined in the vertical plane of symmetry.

22. Steering shall be accomplished by means of a tiller. Tiller may be of any length or shape. Material is optional.

23. Ballast, if used, shall be permanently installed.

24. Fuselage shall be constructed of wood only. (Sitka spruce, oak and plywood—exterior, marine or aircraft—are recommended.) Fiberglas may be added for reenforcement only.

B. RUNNER PLANK

1. Length overall   95″   1″   1″

2. Width at centerline   7″   ½″   ½″

3. Thickness at centerline   1⅜″   ¼″   ¼″

4. Width at ends   5¾″   1¾″   ¼″

5. Thickness at ends   1⅜″   ¼″   ⅜″

6. Cross section is optional

7. Runner plank shall be constructed of wood. Sitka spruce is recommended. Fiberglas may be added.

8. When boat is at rest with skipper *not* aboard, the underside of the runner plank shall be higher at centerline than the underside at outboard ends.

C. MAST

1. Length overall (including hardware)   192″   0″   6″

2. Width—measured from full section above boom jaw area

to mast hound	3¾"	¼"	¼"

3. Thickness—measured from

mast step to mast hound	2¼"	¼"	¼"

4. Only one bolt-rope tunnel is permitted. The bolt-rope tunnel shall be substantially straight with the mast relaxed. Tubing or track prohibited.
5. Cross section profiles are optional. Mast may be hollow.
6. Width and thickness above mast hound is optional.
7. A full length halyard must be installed. An internal halyard is permitted.
8. Devices which prevent or hinder movement of the boom on the mast are prohibited.
9. Mast shall be constructed of wood. Sitka spruce is recommended. Number of laminations is optional. Fiberglas may be added.

D. BOOM

1. Length (from mast)	108"	0"	optional

2. Depth (from outhaul bracket

to 12" from mast)	2¾"	¼"	¼"

3. Thickness (from outhaul

bracket to 12" from mast)	1½"	¼"	¼"

4. Only one bolt-rope tunnel is permitted. The bolt-rope tunnel shall be substantially straight with boom relaxed. Tubing or track prohibited.
5. Cross section profile is optional. Boom may be hollow.
6. Boom jaws are required. Devices which prevent or hinder movement of the boom on the mast are prohibited except for check wire.
7. A ½ inch wide strip shall be painted around the boom in contrasting color. Stripe shall be perpendicular to sail tunnel. Forward edge of the stripe shall be 8', 10" or less from forward inner surface of sail slot, projected fairly to black band.

E. RUNNERS

1. Steel plate type (steel body with stiffening elements).

a. Plate thickness	.25"	.020"	.020"
b. Length	29½"	½"	3½"
c. Height	5"	0"	1"

d. Thickness (contained

by chock)	1"	$\frac{1}{32}$"	$\frac{1}{32}$"

   e. Length, material, location and cross section of stiffening elements are optional.
   f. Method of attaching stiffening elements is optional.
   g. Type of steel plate is optional.
2. Wood type (wood body with attached steel angle, "T" Section or triangular steel section). This means commercially available section. Technical Committee will rule against any special fabrications.

a. Thickness of body	1"	$\frac{1}{32}$"	⅛"
b. Length	36"	0"	6"
c. Height	4⅛"	⅞"	⅛"

d. Thickness contained by

chock	1"	$\frac{1}{32}$"	$\frac{1}{32}$"

   e. Body shall be made of wood. Oak is recommended. Fiberglas may be added.
3. Profile of runner is optional with the exception that front ends

of all runners shall have ⅝" radius or larger.

4. Runner stiffening elements shall not project laterally more than 3" from runner edge.
5. Steering runner shall be equipped with a parking brake.
6. Weight of any individual runner shall not exceed 17 lbs.
7. Method of attaching runner to chock and chock to plank shall be accomplished as shown in plans.
8. Method of providing relative movement of runner with respect to chock shall be as shown in plans.
9. Runner edge angle, camber (crown) and shape of contact line are optional.
10. Each yacht shall be restricted to the use of 3 sets of runners during a regatta.
11. A maximum of four holes, which are not structurally required, may be drilled in each runner. Hole diameters shall not exceed ½" diameter.

F. RUNNER BASE AND CUT (TRACK)
1. Longitudinal distance from pivot axis of steering runner to pivot axis of aft runner   100"   3"   3"
2. Lateral distance between aft runner edges below pivot axis (to be measured with skipper in cockpit in sailing trim)   95"   0"   optional

G. SAIL
1. Material may be of nylon, cotton or dacron. If used, dacron shall be 6.5 oz. cloth manufactured by Howe and Bainbridge with cloth 36" wide or less.
2. Hoist shall be 14 feet or less.
3. Foot shall be 8'10" or less.
4. Leach shall be 14' or less.
5. Girth shall be 5'8" or less excluding bolt rope.
6. The width of the headboard shall be 4" or less. The overall dimension of the head of the sail, including bolt rope shall be 5½" or less.
7. Spacing between battens shall not exceed 36", nor be less than 32".
8. Batten pockets shall lie at 90 degrees plus or minus 5 degrees to the leach.
9. Batten material, length and structural characteristics are optional.
10. Sail may have one row of reef points.
11. A yacht is restricted to the use of one sail in a regatta.
12. Altering the sail characteristics, such as area and camber, during a regatta by any means other than the natural flexing of structural members and positioning the clew grommet on the outhaul bracket are prohibited. This includes reefing. Batten adjustment is excluded.
13. Yacht number and the letters "DN" shall be affixed to each side of the sail. Color of numbers and "DN" shall contrast with sail and be a minimum of 10" high.
14. A transparent window shall not exceed 300 sq. inches.
15. A steel cable, at least 3/64" in dia. shall be attached to headboard, running inside the luff to a point outside the sail at the tack. Lower end of the cable shall form a loop which must be secured to tack pin on boom when under sail. Distance from top of head-

board to center of $\frac{1}{4}$" bolt inserted in the loop shall not exceed 14' with cable straight and under 10 lbs. tension.

16. Sail shall not extend aft of the forward edge of the $\frac{1}{2}$" boom stripe which is located 8'10" from the forward edge of the mast slot.

17. The leach, defined as the distance between the centers of $\frac{1}{4}$" bolts inserted in the head board hole and clew grommet, shall be measured with the sail free of battens and under five pounds tension.

18. The girth (distance between the luff midpoint and the leach midpoint excluding bolt rope) shall be measured with the battens removed and such tension as is required to remove wrinkles. Mid-points are found by folding the sail so holes line up and marking the fold.

H. RIGGING

1. Framing stays are prohibited. Any cable not shown in plans is prohibited.
2. All stays shall be steel cable and shall be $\frac{1}{8}$" or greater in diameter.
3. Halyard shall be steel cable and shall be $\frac{3}{32}$" or greater in diameter.
4. Full length bobstay shall be installed. Bob stay strut must be at least 4" in ht. and anchored on stern block or immediately in front of plank.
5. Tubes and other means of rigid adjustment of stay lengths are permissible.
6. Devices which adjust stay lengths while yacht is under-way are prohibited.
7. Means for rigid adjustment of mast step location are permissible.
8. Means for adjustment of mast step location while yacht is under-way are prohibited.
9. Mast step shall be rigidly mounted on the deck of the fuselage.
10. Mast step shall permit free orientation of mast.
11. Horizontal distance from mast step pivoting point (center of ball) to pivot axis of steering runner.   37"   4"   2"
12. Horizontal distance from pivot axis of steering chock to pivot axis of steering post.   46"   4"   2"
13. Distance from lower mast hound bolt to base of mast $133\frac{1}{2}$"   6"   6"
14. Six sheet blocks shall be installed.
15. 4 sheet blocks shall be installed aft of the rear limit of cockpit floor; 2 on boom; 2 on fuselage.
16. One sheet block shall be located forward on the boom within 1' of mast.
17. One sheet block shall be installed on the tiller post.
18. The sheet must be attached to the boom and pass through all blocks as shown on plans.
19. Blocks must be individual and have fixed positions on fuselage and boom.

I. FITTINGS

1. Diameter of the sheaves of the sheet blocks shall not exceed

4 inches.

2. One of the six required blocks may incorporate a one-way feature.
3. Steering chock may incorporate a shock absorbing feature.
4. Hardware need not conform to plans as long as specifications are not violated and hardware performs the same function that the plan item performs.
5. Side Chock

a. Width of runner slot	$1\frac{1}{32}''$	$\frac{1}{32}''$	$\frac{1}{32}''$
b. Depth of chock	$3''$	$\frac{1}{2}''$	$\frac{1}{8}''$
c. Length of chock	$7''$	$2''$	$\frac{1}{4}''$

6. Mast Step
   a. Height of pivoting point
   (center of ball) above deck $1\frac{3}{8}''$ $\frac{1}{4}''$ $\frac{1}{4}''$
7. Location of halyard catch on mast is optional.
8. Halyard must be capable of lowering and raising the sail with yacht in upright position.
9. Additional fittings to secure halyard to mast are permissible.
10. Only one mast, boom, fuselage and runner plank may be used for an entire regatta, unless broken beyond reasonable repair (as interpreted by Race Committee).

CONSTITUTION
ARTICLE I—NAME AND EMBLEM

The name of this organization shall be the International DN Ice Yacht Racing Association. Its emblem shall be the letters DN, placed on the sail in ten-inch letters, in red or other contrasting color.

ARTICLE II—PURPOSE

The Association's purpose shall be to promote ice yacht racing in this one-design class, in boats built to the Official Specifications, and to sponsor an Annual Regatta.

ARTICLE III—ORGANIZATION AND FISCAL YEAR

The Association is one of individual members, acting through general membership meetings, and through the Governing Committee. The fiscal year shall be April 1 through March 31.

ARTICLE IV—DUES AND FEES

Association dues and entrance fee to the Annual Regatta shall be fixed by the By-Laws.

ARTICLE V—MEMBERSHIP

There shall be three classes of membership, as follows:
  A. Active: Any owner or part-owner of a DN, in good standing. Privileges are to sail in the Annual Regatta, vote on the Association's affairs, receive all Association communications, and hold office.
  B. Associate: Any non-DN-owner interested in the affairs of the Association, in good standing. Privileges are to receive all Association communications.
  C. Inactive: Any Active or Associate member who has not paid dues for the current year by the time of the Annual Regatta will no longer be considered a member in good standing, and will be transferred to Inactive status. There are no privileges.

Members must be Corinthians, and power to accept or reject applications for membership is vested in the Governing Committee.

ARTICLE VI—ELECTION AND DUTIES OF OFFICERS

A Commodore, Vice Commodore, and Secretary-Treasurer shall be elected at the Annual Meeting, and shall take office on April 1. Terms of office expire the following March 31. Each shall be nominated and voted upon in the order named above. The candidate receiving the greatest number of votes shall be considered elected.

Duties are as follows:

A. Commodore: To be chief executive, preside at all meetings, be chairman of the Governing Committee, rule on procedure and jurisdiction, summarize decisions, appoint special committees, authorize payment of bills.

B. Vice-Commodore: To officiate in the absence of the Commodore.

C. Secretary-Treasurer: To handle system of forms; keep minutes and all other Association records, including membership and yacht registration; award numbers; publish an annual directory; maintain Association funds in a checking account; disburse funds on order of the Commodore; send reports and notices to the membership. He shall bring all records up to date, complete business pending from the Annual Meeting, complete an annual financial report as of March 31, and shall transmit all Association records to his successor as soon as possible after March 31.

ARTICLE VII—GOVERNING COMMITTEE

The Governing Committee consists of the three Officers, acting as a group. Its powers are to render final decisions on appeal, sanction or prohibit races in the Annual Regatta, accept or reject membership applications, approve the Race Committee for the Annual Regatta, and perform other duties mentioned in the By-Laws.

The Governing Committee may initiate changes in the Constitution, By-Laws, Official Specifications, or Racing Rules by proposing such changes to the entire membership at the Annual Meeting, or by mail. Membership vote is required for enactment of all proposed changes. Otherwise, the Governing Committee may not change or modify any of the above documents, although it has the power to interpret them.

ARTICLE VIII—MEETINGS AND QUORUM

The Annual Meeting shall be held during and in the vicinity of the Annual Regatta, if possible. Special meetings may be called on the order of the Governing Committee or upon demand in writing by twenty-five per cent of the membership. Exact time and place of all meetings shall be fixed by the Governing Committee. If a special meeting is called the purpose thereof must be stated in such form as to permit voting by mail, and no other business may be transacted.

A quorum at a meeting is any number present. However, if less than twenty percent of the then-paid membership is present, all action must be ratified (unless rejected) by a mail vote. In addition, any action requiring a majority of two-thirds (such as amendments to Constitution or By-Laws, or changes in the Official Specifications or Racing Rules) shall be put to a mail vote, regardless of the number present at the Annual Meeting.

All meetings shall be conducted according to Roberts' *Rules of Order.*

ARTICLE IX—VOTING

A majority of the votes cast shall be determining on all questions not otherwise stipulated, and the chair (if in a meeting) shall cast the deciding vote in case of a tie. The chair also has the power to fix a time limit on speakers and discussion of motions.

ARTICLE X—OFFICIAL SPECIFICATIONS

Requirements for the yacht, sail, and attached equipment shall be set forth in the *Official Specifications of the DN Ice Yacht.* They are the sole rules for meeting equipment specifications, and the Official Plans are only a suggested guide to building.

The Official Specifications shall be enforced in two ways. First, any contestant, or a Judge or Race Committee member at the Annual Regatta may file a protest against any competing yacht. Secondly, the Race Committee shall measure the first five place-winning pachts at the conclusion of the Annual Regatta.

ARTICLE XI—AMENDMENTS AND CHANGES

Amendments to the Constitution or By-Laws, and changes in the Official Specifications or the Racing Rules, may be made only after approval of the membership by a mail vote. A two-thirds majority of the votes cast is required.

Changes in the Official Specifications shall become effective for the following season only if approved by July 1. Otherwise they shall become effective for the next following season.

ARTICLE XII—TECHNICAL COMMITTEE

The Technical Committee shall consist of five members. One new member shall be elected each year at the Annual meeting for a term of five years. Upon resignation prior to five years, a replacement member shall be elected at the Annual meeting to serve the unexpired term. Term of office will begin April 1 and expire March 31 of the appropriate year. Each year the committee shall elect from its membership a chairman to serve until March 31 of the following year. The chairman shall report to the Governing Committee on all recommendations of the Technical Committee.

The committee may *initiate* changes in the Official Specifications by proposing such changes to the Governing Committee, who may submit them to the membership on a mail ballot requiring ⅔ majority for approval.

The committee shall, upon the *request* of any member, or at the direction of the Governing Committee, provide interpretation of the Official Specifications. These findings shall be published in Association Newsletters. Such interpretations shall prevail as Supplements to the Official Specifications unless and until voided by a simple majority vote via mail ballot.

If a committee seat becomes vacant for any reason the Commodore may appoint a replacement until the next Annual Meeting.

Bylaws
General

1. Dues for Active and Associate members are $2.00 annually, payable December 1 to the Secretary-Treasurer.
2. An entry fee of $5.00 shall be charged all members entering the Annual Regatta. Such fees go to the host club.
3. Each yacht shall be assigned a number the Secretary-Treasurer, upon application by the member. The application shall include name and address of the owner, present number (if a used boat), name of builder, year built, and signed certification that the yacht complies with the Official Specifications as of the application date. The number shall appear on the sail, in ten-inch figures.
4. An annual Membership Directory shall be published by November 1, and will include all Active and Associate members of the preceding year, plus members added since March 31.

Annual Regatta

1. The Association shall hold an Annual Regatta which shall be conducted by an ice yacht club selected at the previous Annual Meet-

ing, but if such Club cannot hold the regatta on the scheduled date or one week thereafter, the regatta may be transferred by the Governing Committee.

2. To enter, a yacht must be the bonafide property of an Association member, or shall have been chartered in good faith for a period of not less than thirty days. The charterer shall be deemed the owner. In addition, the yacht must conform to the Official Specifications, and dues for the current year must be paid.

3. The club conducting the regatta shall be responsible for its proper management and shall select starters, scorers, mark-watchers, and a Race Committee. These officials are not required to be members of the Association but should be familiar with ice yacht racing. If the club conducting the regatta desires assistance in conducting it the commodore shall provide it.

4. The Race Committee shall see that all skippers are properly informed before starting the regatta. There shall be a Skipper's Meeting before the first race, time and place to be announced by mail prior to the regatta week-end.

5. The regatta shall be held on a Consecutive Saturday or Sunday. It shall consist of five races, subject to the following conditions:
   a. Three races must be completed to complete the regatta.
   b. All races shall be four miles in length, and the course shall be windward-and-return.
   c. Lap time limit shall be nine minutes per mile for any yacht to complete each lap—for details see NIA Rules Part II, para. G-1-d.
   d. Any yacht not finishing within thirty minutes of the first yacht shall be scored DNF (Did Not Finish).
   e. Twenty Minutes must elapse from the time of the last boat to finish to the start of the next race.
   f. No race may be started after 4:30 P.M.
   g. No more than three races may be held in one day.

6. The Race Committee may postpone any race if they consider conditions unsafe.

7. Except in emergencies (to be determined by the Race Committee), the same person must sail a yacht throughout a regatta.

8. Failure to use the parking brake at any time that the yacht is left unattended with sail up, may result in disqualification for entire Regatta if damage or injury results and the Race Committee deems it appropriate.

9. Hard Surfaced, suitably padded headgear (crash helmet) *must* be worn while racing in the Annual Regatta, and is recommended for all regattas.

10. A yacht may be disqualified for violation of any written rule of the Association or any NIA Racing Rule. Protests shall be made and heard according to NIA procedure (Part V).

11. Appeal from a decision of the Race Committee may be made to the Governing Committee, who may in turn permit an appeal to the NIA for interpretation.

12. If three races have not been completed, races already sailed shall be cancelled and the Governing Committee shall reschedule the Regatta. A skipper who did not enter on the original weekend may enter the rescheduled Regatta. Entry fees will not be refunded, nor will a skipper be required to pay more than once. If a different club hosts the postponed Regatta, the originally-scheduled club shall

transfer Regatta trophies and remaining Regatta funds to the other club.
13. The Race Committee chairman of the host club shall furnish the Secretary-Treasurer with a copy of the final results, in detail.

RACING RULES

The current racing rules of the National Iceboat Authority (as amended and interpreted through appeal decisions) shall prevail in all IDNYRA regattas. It is imperative that all skippers obtain a copy of these Racing Rules and learn them thoroughly. The rules were developed for unique problems in safe iceboat racing and therefore differ slightly from the rules that prevail in yacht racing. Copies may be obtained for 50¢ from the Secretary of the N.I.A., 6615 N. Seoux Avenue, Chicago 46, Illinois.

NATIONAL ICEBOAT AUTHORITY

The officers of the IDNYRA recommend that DN members join the N.I.A. Membership costs $2.00 and includes the Racing Rules (and all amendments), notices of Appeals Decisions, etc. Additional levies are made only when the funds are needed.

Glossary of Terms

APPARENT WIND—Angle of the resultant wind to the hull centerline while moving. Same as relative wind

ARROW—A two-place one-design iceboat

BATTEN—Thin, flexible, flat strip of wood used to stiffen a sail

BEAR OFF—To change heading in a direction away from the wind. Opposite from head up

BEAT—To tack upwind

BLACK ICE—Newly frozen, transparent ice

BLOCKS—Pulleys

BOB STAY—A cable going lengthwise over a strut under the hull to strengthen it

BOOM—The horizontal rigid member, pivoted to the mast and attached to the lower edge of the sail

BRAKE, HAND—A pivoted lever attached to hull or runner plank the lower end of which scratches to use to slow or stop the boat

BRAKE, PARKING—Device on a runner that folds under the runner when boat is parked to keep it from sliding on the ice

CHOCKS—The fittings into which the runners are fastened

CLEW—The lower, back corner of the sail

CLOSE-HAULED—Sailing with boom close to hull centerline

COME ABOUT—To change from port to starboard tack or vice versa. Synonymous with tack in this meaning

CREEPER—Spiked devices on shoes to keep from slipping on ice

DN—A small, popular one-design racing iceboat

DOWN HAUL—A cable or fitting to pull the front of boom downward on the mast to tighten the sail

FORESTAY—Cable from the hound to the front of the hull, also called bowstay

GIVE WAY—Turn away from best heading because of right of way of another boat

HALYARD—The cable and/or rope used to raise the sail on the mast

HEADBOARD—The stiff section at the top of the sail where the halyard attaches

HEADING—The angle between the long axis of the hull and the wind or the race course centerline

HEAD UP—To change heading closer into the wind

HIKE—To ride on steering and one plank runner

HOUND—The fitting on the mast to which the shrouds and forestay attach

ICE YACHT—Same as iceboat, not necessarily bigger

JIBE—To turn from one diagonal downwind heading to the opposite side

KEEP CLEAR—Stay out of the path of another boat

LEE—On the sheltered side from the wind; downwind

LEECH—The free, rear edge of the sail

LEEWARD—In direction of wind

LUFF—To let the sail flap or lose shape in the wind. The edge of the sail against the mast

MARKER or MARK—The pylon on the ice that defines the race course

OFF-THE-WIND—To turn away from the wind direction

OFF-THE-WIND HEADING—A heading of more than 90° from true wind direction

ON-THE-WIND HEADING—A heading of less than 90° from true wind direction

OVERLAP—When any part of one boat is forward up the back most part of another boat when both are running close together on the same heading

PAY SHEET—To let out the sheet

PEEL OFF—To change from a tack heading smoothly through crosswind to a reach

PINCH—To tack very close into the wind

PORT TACK—Sailing with wind coming from the port, or left side. The boom will be on the right side

RAKE—The backward lean of an iceboat mast

REACH—To sail approximately crosswind. A broad reach is to sail at a heading between crosswind and downwind

RENEGADE—A one-design, single-place Skeeter

RIFT—A large crack in the ice with water in between

ROACH—The part of the sail aft of the triangle formed by the mast and boom

ROUND UP—To curve into the wind and stop

RUNNER PLANK— (Plank) The long athwartship member to which the hull and two parallel runners are attached

RUNNERS—The metal blades on which the iceboat rides on the ice

SCOOTER—An iceboat that can sail in water or on ice

SHEET—The line that is used to change the sail angle

SHEET IN—To pull in the sheet

SHROUDS—The cables from the hound on the mast to the springboard

SKATE SAIL—A kitelike sail that the sailor holds onto while on skates

SKEETER—A front-steering racing iceboat with not over 75 square feet of sail

SLOP—The amount of sideways motion of the mast permitted by loose shrouds

SPRINGBOARD—A flexible section forward of the point on the hull where the forestay is attached which mounts the steering runner

SPLIT TACK—When one boat tacks to starboard and another to port. On a start when half the boats start on one tack and the other half the other

STARBOARD TACK—Sailing with wind coming from the starboard or right side. The boom will be on the left side

TACK—A very ambiguous term in iceboating. It means sailing close hauled either upwind or downwind. Also to switch from one heading diagonally upwind to a similar heading on the opposite diagonal. Also to lower forward corner of the sail

TELLTALE—Ribbon attached to stay or pivoted feather or vane to show direction of relative wind

TILLER—A lever usually held in the skipper's hand for steering

VECTOR—An arrowlike symbol representing the direction and speed or force of something

VIKING—A 2-place, one-design iceboat

(To) WEATHER—Toward the wind, windward

WHITE ICE—Ice with air bubbles in it made from frozen slush

WINDWARD—Into the wind or on the side on which the wind blows

WIND DIRECTION—The direction from which the wind comes. A north wind blows snow from north to south

YANKEE—A two-place one-design Skeeter

Index